The Body Coach Series

Dynamic Dumbbell Training

The Ultimate Guide to Strength and Power Training with
Australia's Body Coach®

Paul Collins

Meyer & Meyer Sport

British Library Cataloguing in Publication Data
A catalogue record for this book is available from the British Library

Paul Collins
Dynamic Dumbbell Training
Maidenhead: Meyer & Meyer Sport (UK) Ltd., 2011
ISBN 978-1-84126-310-6

© 2011 Paul Collins (text & photos)
and Meyer & Meyer Sport (UK) Ltd. (Layout)
Aachen, Auckland, Beirut, Budapest, Cairo, Cape Town, Dubai, Graz, Indianapolis,
Maidenhead, Melbourne, Olten, Singapore, Tehran, Toronto
Member of the World
Sport Publishers' Association (WSPA)
www.w-s-p-a.org

Printed and bound by: B.O.S.S Druck und Medien GmbH, Germany
ISBN 978-1-84126-310-6
E-Mail: info@m-m-sports.com
www.m-m-sports.com

Contents

Trademarks
Body Coach®, The Body Coach®, Fastfeet®, Quickfeet®, Speedhoop®, Posturefit®, Spinal Unloading Block®, 3 Hour Rule®, Australia's Personal Trainer™, Speed for Sport™, Collins-Technique™, Coach Collins™, Collins Lateral Fly™, 20-40-60 Exercise Principle™, Core-in Motion Method™ (CIMM™); Abdominal Wheel System™, GTS™ Grid Training System™ and 3B's Principle™ are trademarks of Paul Collins.

About the Author

Paul Collins, Australia's Personal Trainer™ is founder of The Body Coach® fitness products, books, DVDs and educational coaching systems – helping people to get fit, lose weight, look good and feel great. Coaching since age 14, Paul has personally trained world-class athletes and teams in a variety of sports from Track and Field, Squash, Rugby, Golf, Soccer and Tennis to members of the Australian World Championship Karate Team, Manly 1st Grade Rugby Union Team and members of the world-renowned Australian Olympic and Paralympic Swimming teams. Paul is an outstanding athlete is his own right, having played grade rugby league in the national competition, an A-grade squash player, National Budokan Karate Champion and NSW State Masters Athletics Track & Field Champion.

A recipient of the prestigious 'Fitness Instructor of the Year Award' in Australia, Paul is regarded by his peers as the 'Trainers' Trainer' having educated thousands of fitness instructors and personal trainers and appearing in TV, radio and print media internationally. Over the past decade, Paul has presented to national sporting bodies including the Australian Track and Field Coaching Association, Australia Swimming Coaches and Teachers Association, Australian Rugby League, Australian Karate Federation and the Australian Fitness Industry as well as travelling to present a highly entertaining series of Corporate Health & Wellbeing Seminars for companies focused on a Body for Success™ in Life and in Business.

Paul holds a Bachelor of Physical Education degree from the Australian College of Physical Education. He is also a Certified Trainer and Assessor, Strength and Conditioning Coach with the Australian Sports Commission and Olympic Weight Lifting Club Power Coach with the Australian Weightlifting Federation. As a Certified Personal Trainer with Fitness Australia, Paul combines over two decades of experience as a talented athlete, coach and mentor for people of all age groups and ability levels in achieving their optimal potential.

In his free time, Paul enjoys competing in track and field, travelling, food and movies. He resides in Sydney, Australia

For more details visit: www.thebodycoach.com

A Word from The Body Coach®

For any person looking at increasing their muscular size, strength and tone and coordination as well as explosive power for improving general fitness and athletic performance – then *Dynamic Dumbbell Training* is the ultimate training guide for you. Let me explain!

Every piece of exercise equipment in the gym serves a purpose, but none so more than the dumbbell, commonly referred to as free weights or hand weights. *Dynamic Dumbbell Training* is more beneficial than exercise machines and barbells because exercises work on activating smaller stabilizing muscle groups to control the movement pattern through various planes of movement – increasing muscular activation and movement control. This means that you are no longer governed by the fixed position or limited range, instead you are drawn into the training process through better muscular coordination and control of both deep core and larger muscle group involvement aimed at replicating daily lifestyle or sport-specific movement patterns more accurately and ultimately improving Central Nervous System (CNS) recruitment, muscular coordination and fat loss.

In traditional strength training, dumbbells have been used to strengthen or isolate a muscle group or series of muscle groups in a fixed or stationary position standing or whilst lying, kneeling or sitting on a bench. With the introduction of *Dynamic Dumbbell Training* I aim to take you one step further with my breakthrough **3-Stage Dynamic Dumbbell Training System™:**

Stage 1: Strength
Stage 2: Functional
Stage 3: Power

Each stage aims to progress you through a series of progressive strength and 'Sports-Specific' powerful movement patterns aimed at improving everyday lifestyle and athletic movement patterns on top of your strength gains.

This means that whilst I will be helping you establish a solid strength foundation through traditional dumbbell training methods, I will also be combining this with more functional and dynamic movement patterns performed in an athletic position on one's feet or an unstable environment such as sitting or lying on a **fitness ball** or using a **Kettlebell** and **Olympic Lifting** techniques for increased kinesthetic awareness, core stability and sports specificity through speed of movement and explosive power development.

Dynamic Dumbbell Training is loaded with exercise information beneficial for any athlete, exercise enthusiast, coach or trainer at any level. It contains all the fundamental guidelines for participating in a safe and efficient strength-training program, whilst sequencing exercises towards the development of more explosive power through my **3-Stage Dynamic Dumbbell Training System™**. This approach will ensure you gain good foundational strength, increased muscle mass and strength endurance whilst also challenging your body with more functional and dynamic movement patterns for achieving the ultimate athletic body.

Dynamic Dumbbell Training also aims to take the guesswork out of training by providing you with specific exercises and training routines. So, whilst there may be thousands of dumbbell exercises available, this often only brings confusion into the process; whereas 'my objective' is to bring specificity and focus into your weekly training program for a better learning experience and greater results with the Body Coach® Strength Training System! This way you know what you're doing and when, which is an important element for me as a coach – ensuring you are guided all the way!

I look forward to working with you!
Paul Collins
The Body Coach®

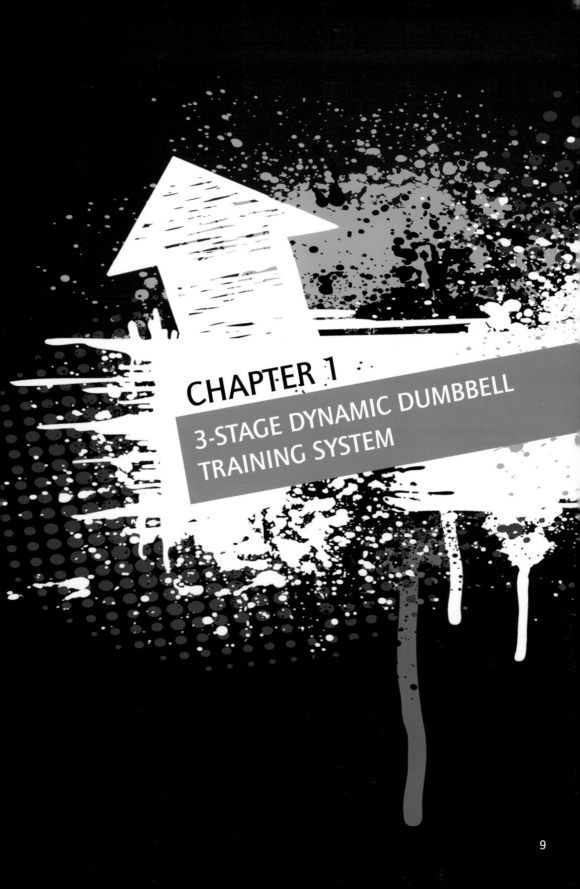

CHAPTER 1

3-STAGE DYNAMIC DUMBBELL TRAINING SYSTEM

Every good exercise program starts with a method upon which training principles are based. In my book, *Awesome Abs*, I devised a 5-Phase Abdominal Training System for maximizing your core potential. In, *Speed for Sport*™ I devised a 6-Stage Fastfeet® Training Model for maximizing your speed potential. In *Functional Fitness* I devised a Functional Fitness Method (FFM) with '6- Key Movement Patterns' that aim to provide a balance of muscular strength, fitness and mobility throughout multiple planes of motion. In *Strength Training for Men*, I have devised the 5-Phase Core-Strength to Power Conversion Training System™ which aims to improve fundamental core-strength, mobility and coordination required for Olympic Lifting and power gains. In *Core-Fitness*, I introduced a new approach focused on cavity based training along with the Core-in-Motion Method™ for improved muscular control in functional athletic positions. In *Athletic Abs*, I introduced the Top 10 abdominal exercises of all time using the revolutionary Abdominal Wheel System™. And now, in this book I have developed a 3-Stage Dynamic Dumbbell Training System™ that progresses you through stages of strength, function and power training.

3-Stage Progression

A method of progression in any training program needs to first be established to enable one to know where to start as well as where one needs to progress to. The innovative 3-Stage progression applied here allows the participant time to establish appropriate strength throughout the body, its muscles, joints, energy and nervous systems and progressively adapt to new functional and more powerful movement patterns for optimal athletic gains. Below are the 3 stages involved:

3-Stage Dynamic Dumbbell Training System™

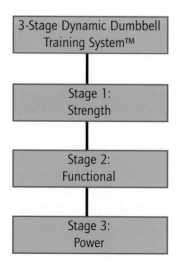

Stage 1: Strength

The general strength preparation phase is based on a diverse range of strength movement exercises using dumbbells that aim to improve muscle coordination and endurance and neural adaptation, before progressing onto the goal of increasing the cross-sectional area of muscle and ultimately maximum strength. The main exercises provided in Stage 1 involve individual isolated exercises as well as compound movement exercises that target multiple muscle groups used in sports and for gaining overall athleticism. This stage includes exercise instruction in technique and breathing for increasing body awareness and maximizing muscular strength and endurance.

Stage 2: Functional

As general strength improves, more functional-based exercises can be added into the program for challenging strength and coordination. These exercises should not be performed alone, but rather in association with Stage 1 exercises, as in many instances the weight being lifted is reduced in comparison to Stage 1 due to the functional movement pattern and coordination required. As movement function and control improves, the dumbbell weight used is increased as well as the repetitions (or time) and sets to heighten the challenge – with quality of movement being the main objective here.

Stage 3: Power

After developing strength and general functional movement patterns, your goal is to convert this into power. In Stage 3 we concentrate on exercises that link two or more strength foundation exercises together that form a part or sequence or a simulated Olympic Lifting style movement using dumbbells – generating a high level of speed, force and power. The objective here is to never sacrifice lifting technique for a heavier weight and ensure the strength and functional movement patterns are in place prior to implementing in Stage 3. This is essential for building technique and muscular coordination of more powerful lifts together with the continual adaptation of the neuromuscular framework as part of a power progression using sub-maximal loads for mastering technique before increasing loads.

Program Design

One of the most important elements of any sport or activity is a well-designed strength-training program. With the 3 stages now in place, a series of progressive strength training programs have been created to help guide you towards your goal. As appropriate strength gains require the attention of a number of training variables, being able to identifying and apply the 'Anatomy of Movement' on the following pages helps you to progress in your complete knowledge and understanding of training requirements and optimal performance.

Anatomy of Movement

Strength training has a variety of terms used to describe the movement patterns, muscle contractions and various descriptions when exercising. Simple terms often become more complex as training progresses which can seem confusing at times, although the more you get involved the more knowledge and understanding you'll have of your body. In this chapter, I will outline many of the important key words used throughout this book and also in a gym or sports training environment.

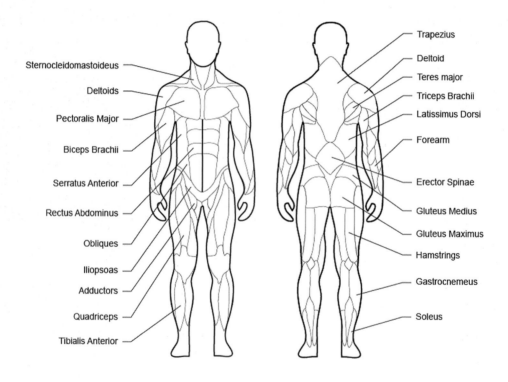

Front view labels:
- Sternocleidomastoideus
- Deltoids
- Pectoralis Major
- Biceps Brachii
- Serratus Anterior
- Rectus Abdominus
- Obliques
- Iliopsoas
- Adductors
- Quadriceps
- Tibialis Anterior

Back view labels:
- Trapezius
- Deltoid
- Teres major
- Triceps Brachii
- Latissimus Dorsi
- Forearm
- Erector Spinae
- Gluteus Medius
- Gluteus Maximus
- Hamstrings
- Gastrocnemeus
- Soleus

Muscle Chart

Muscle	Origin	Insertion	Function	Location
Abductors	Ilium	Femur	Brings hip away from body.	Front and rear side of hip region; TFL, Gluteus medius and minimus
Adductors	Pubis	Femur	Brings leg back to and across body.	Inside of upper leg (groin area)
Biceps brachii	Scapula	Radius and Ulna	Flexes elbow and moves forearm.	Front side of upper arm
Brachialis	Humerus and Septa	Coronoid process and Ulna	Flexes elbow.	Forearm
Brachioradialis	Humerus and Septum	Radius	Flexes and rotates elbow.	Forearm
Deltoid	Clavicle, Deltoid tuberosity, Acromion and Scapula	Deltoid tuberosity (Humerus)	Raises and rotates arm in all directions.	Shoulders
Erector spinae	Sacrum and Ilium	Upper Thoracic vertebrae	Extends spine and trunk back.	Back region (along spine)
Gastrocnemius	Femur Lower leg - back	Calcaneum (by Achilles tendon)	Raises heel when leg is straight.	Rear side of lower leg (calf muscle)
Gluteus maximus	Ilium	Femur	Moves hips forward.	Buttock region (rear side of hip)
Hamstrings (made of 3 muscles): 1. Biceps femoris 2. Semitendinosus 3. Semimembranosus	1. Ischium 2. Ischium 3. Ischium	1. Fibula and Femur 2. Tibia 3. Tibia	1. Bends knee. 2. Bends knee. 3. Bends knee.	Rear side of upper leg
Iliopsoas	Ilium, Sacrum, Thoracic and Lumbar vertebrae	Femur	Moves hips backwards.	Deep hip flexors
Latissimus dorsi	Lower Thoracic, Lumbar vertebrae and Sacrum	Humerus	Brings shoulders and arms back to body.	Rear sides of mid to upper back

13

Pectoralis major and minor	Sternum	Humerus	Moves Humerus (arm) to chest.	Chest region
Quadriceps (made of 4 muscles): 1. Rectus femoris 2. Vastus lateralis 3. Vastus medialis 4. Vastus intermedius	1. Ilium 2. Femur 3. Femur 4. Femur	Tibia (Patellar tendon)	1. Extends leg out. 2. Extends knee. 3. Extends knee. 4. Extends knee.	Front side of upper leg (thigh)
Rectus abdominis	Costal cartilages, Medial inferiorcostal	Margin and Xiphoid	Brings trunk forward, and aids expiration.	Abdominal region
Rhomboids	Upper Thoracic vertebrae	Scapula	Pulls back Scapula (shoulder blades).	Upper back
Soleus (calf muscles)	Tibia and Fibula	Calcaneum (by Achilles tendon)	Raises heel when leg is bent.	Rear side of lower leg (calf muscle)
Tibialis anterior	Tibia	Metatarsal (large toe)	Raises front of foot.	Front side of lower leg
Trapezius	Starts at base of skull. Ends at last thoracic vertebra.	Scapula and clavicle elevation.	Elevates and lowers pectoral girdle. Also moves scapula towards the spine.	Neck and shoulder region
Triceps	Brachi, Scapula and Humerus	Olecranon process (elbow)	Extends forearm.	Rear side of upper arm

Anatomical Planes

The body itself is divided into four anatomical planes – Sagittal, Frontal, Horizontal and Oblique. The Sagittal plane divides the body down the center or vertically. The Frontal plane divides the body from front to back. The Horizontal plane divides upper and lower whilst the Oblique plane is diagonal. The table below lists the anatomical term and the corresponding description.

ANATOMICAL TERM	DESCRIPTION
Anterior	Front
Medial	Inside
Posterior	Rear
Lateral	Outside
Supine	Face up
Unilateral	One side
Bilateral	Both sides
Prone	Face down
Superior	Upper
Inferior	Lower

Each of the movements of the muscles of the body is described by the following terms:

- Abductor – Moves a limb away from the midline
- Adductor – Moves a limb toward the midline
- Extensor – Increases the angle at a joint (extends a limb)
- Flexor – Decreases the angle at a joint (flexes a limb)
- Pronator – Turns a limb to face downwards
- Supinator – Turns a limb to face upwards
- Rotator – Rotates a limb

Joint Actions

Muscular joints of the body provide a fulcrum point for muscles to be worked. There are six types of joint actions. In the table below I will describe the movement and example exercise:

EXAMPLE MOVEMENT	JOINT ACTION	MOVEMENT DESCRIPTION
Biceps Curl	Flexion	Decreasing joint angle by bending arm and raising dumbbell
Leg Extension	Extension	Increasing joint angle by lowering and straightening arm after curling
Deltoid Lateral Raises	Abduction	Movement away from the body midline
Chest Flyes	Adduction	Movement toward the body midline – bringing the dumbbells together up overhead from a lying position on back
Twisting the Arm	Rotation	Rotation about an axis
Circling the arm around	Circumduction	360-degree rotation

Types of Muscle Contraction

While it is known that muscle fibers can only contract and shorten, as a whole they can develop a force in more than one way as shown below:

Isometric   •   Where the muscle tension and muscle length remain constant
Concentric   •   Where the muscles shorten as the fibers contract
Eccentric   •   Where the muscles lengthen as tension develops
Isokinetic   •   Where the muscle contracts though its full range of movement

In each exercise there are four main functions of the associated muscles:

1. **Agonists** (prime movers) - generally refers to the muscle we are exercising.
2. **Antagonists** - the opposing muscle acting in contrast to the agonist.
3. **Stabilizers** - hold a joint in place so that the exercise may be performed. The stabilizer muscles are not necessarily moving during exercise, but provide stationary support.
4. **Assistors** - help the Agonist muscle doing the work.

The following table lists muscles and their opposing counterparts. These columns are reversed when exercising muscle on the right hand column; for example, the Antagonist becomes the Agonist and visa versa:

AGONIST (Prime Mover)	ANTAGONIST
Biceps	Triceps
Deltoids	Latissimus dorsi
Pectoralis major	Trapezius/Rhomboids
Rectus abdominis	Erector spinae
Iliopsoas	Gluteus maximus
Hip Adductor	Gluteus medius
Quadriceps	Hamstrings
Tibialis anterior	Gastrocnemius

In prescribing various exercises and training programs, it is important to have muscle balance to prevent injury. Muscular balance refers to the relationship between the Agonist and Antagonist. If the Agonist is much stronger than the Antagonist (or visa versa) the Agonist can overpower the Antagonist and lead to possible injury. To ensure muscular balance is achieved, a series of exercise tests need to be performed to find one's strengths and weaknesses from which appropriate programming can be designed.

Exercise Terminology

Exercise terminology is separated into 3 key areas:

1. **Isolated** - is an exercise that involves just one discernible joint movement.
2. **Compound** - relates to an exercise that involves two or more joint movements.
3. **Static** - refers to holding a muscle in a static position relative to the desired body position.

Isolated and Compound Movements

All exercises vary in their movement mechanics. Isolated exercises refer to single joint exercises that target a specific muscle group, for example, the biceps arm curl exercise (elbow joint) specifically targets the biceps muscle group of the upper arm. On the other hand, compound exercises involve more than one joint such as movement at the ankle, knee, and hip with an exercise such as a squat. In most instances, the larger muscle groups incorporating larger muscle groups should always form the basis of your routine. Common compound movements are squats, presses, pull-ups and rows, as well as the Olympic Lifts and their assistance exercises (such as pulls, presses, shrugs on toes).

Isolated Exercise – Biceps Curl   Compound Exercise – Squat

Ideally more difficult movements which use many joints and muscles are placed first in the workout, while simpler isolated exercises which move only one joint (such as biceps curls) are placed towards the end. Usually exercises for torso musculature (abdominals, obliques, lower back) are also placed at the end in order to ensure that they are fresh for more demanding exercises in the beginning, and able to provide as much torso support as possible.

CHAPTER 2
DUMBBELL PREPARATION

When you're looking for a piece of exercise equipment that offers the body a unique challenge, you can't look past a pair of dumbbells and for good reason. They're portable and allow you to work different muscles at different angles for a complete full body workout. The challenge itself comes from the weight of the dumbbells generally being held in both hands whilst being pulled, pushed or raised through various angles or ranges of motion. In other cases, the dumbbells are simply used to add extra weight to a movement such as a squat exercise and even more challenging squat with a overhead dumbbell press, right through to exercises that ignite the Central Nervous System (CNS) with simulated Olympic-Lifting movements that aim to increase maximal strength and power development. Whichever the case you can be assured that you'll also be challenging your center of gravity and strengthening your inner core.

Types of Dumbbells

We now live in a day and age where the latest engineering technology makes exercise more compact, cost effective and efficient. Such is the case of the new dumbbell block training system that encompasses a set or series of dumbbells formed into an adjustable weighted block where a specific weight can be chosen through the simple adjustment of a pin. The more traditional types of dumbbells include old school round-end-molded dumbbells, hexagon head shapes and fixed plate types generally found at a gym as a set on a rack ranging in weight from increments of 2.5kg right up to 60kg or more (1kg = 2.2 pounds). Most importantly, you also have a more cost efficient adjustable type home kit available where weight plates can be added to a dumbbell handle and a threaded screw-on or spin-lock collar or spring-loaded clips used to hold the plates in place. This is important to understand because different exercises require different weights. So, no matter what your budget or situation you'll find a pair or series of pairs, adjustable set or block type to suit your training needs.

Training Accessories

The major accessories generally used in line with dumbbell training include an **adjustable bench** that allows a lying pattern on a flat, incline or decline surface. If working out at home, this takes away the need for three individual benches because adjustments can be made to suit each exercise on this one bench. On the other hand a more portable and cost-effective training accessory is the **fitness ball** commonly referred to as a Swiss ball, physio ball or stability ball. My recommendation here is that you must invest in a quality anti-burst type fitness ball with a weight rating of 500kg or more to ensure effective support, movement and safety.

So, whether you have the luxury of working out in a gym with a full set of fixed plate dumbbells along with flat, incline and decline benches as well as additional benches such as the high bench, preacher curl or lower back raise; or you simply work out at home with an adjustable set of dumbbells and a fitness ball – either way you have the ingredients to achieve great results!

Applying the 3B's Principle™

Every exercise has a number of key elements to consider when setting up and performing a movement. Applying correct technique from the onset will help establish good form that is ultimately maintained until the number of repetitions or set is completed. After reviewing Anatomy of Movement, the key elements required in order to maintain good body position whilst exercising form part of a simple exercise set-up phrase I've termed the **3B's Principle™**:

1. Brace

Activating and bracing your abdominal (core) muscles whilst exercising is important because it helps increase awareness of your body position as well as helping unload any stress placed on the lower back region.

2. Breath

In dumbbell training, you **breathe out** when you exert a force – such as pushing the dumbbells overhead in the shoulder press exercise or rising up straight from a squat position. You then **breathe in** with recovery – such as lower the dumbbells back down from overhead or lowering the body and bending the legs when performing a squat. Breathing should remain constant throughout each exercise.

3. Body Position

To complete the 3B's Principle™, the third 'B' relates to one's ability to hold a good body position and technique with each exercise. In all exercises, ensure good head and neck, spine and pelvic alignment is maintained at all times with the rest of the body. The overall focus of each exercise should therefore be on quality of the movement.

So, next time you perform any exercise, simply apply the 3B's Principle™ from start to finish in order maintain correct technique and body posture to help maximize your strength gains.

Functional Warm-up

As the scientific knowledge and understanding of our body and training practices improve, it seems a Functional (or Dynamic) Warm-up plays a number of crucial roles towards improving the quality of movement and athletic performance:

- Gradually increasing your heart rate and core body temperature by performing activities on the move.
- Setting your muscular and nervous systems in motion.

- Working muscles and joints through an appropriate range of movement.
- Heightening the ability of your muscles to contract and be ready for activities that follow reducing the risk of injury.
- Allowing you to warm up your muscles so that they are ready to work at full speed.
- Improving physical and mental alertness by setting a tone to follow for the rest of the session.
- Incorporating a routine of exercises to improve balance, technique, coordination and range of movement.
- Improving athleticism through good technique and range of motion.

Muscles that are warm and without movement restrictions ensure movement quality of the strength training exercises that follow. This is maximized when applying the 3B's Principle™ with each exercise to ensure good body posture whilst helping maximize strength, functional and power gains.

Warm-up Progression

The first stage of a good warm-up is increasing the heart rate and muscle temperature through cardiovascular movement such as walking or a light jog; or using a stationary bike or rowing machine, treadmill or something similar for approximately 5-10 minutes. This also helps to bring one's mindset to the exercise program that follows.

The second stage focuses on range of movement and control of each joint. This is achieved by combining a dynamic movement through a range of motion followed by brief stretch or series of stretches whilst the muscle is warm, except where a joint is hypermobile and a stability approach is required for better muscle control (no stretching). During this period you can also gauge whether specific muscles require further stretching or muscle control techniques. This pattern is demonstrated below as part of the Coach Collins™ Warm-up Sequence. (Also refer to my Speed for Sport™ book.)

Coach Collins™ Warm-up Sequence Cycle 1

Instructions:
Complete the following warm-up sequence from 1-8 before repeating drills on opposite leg for a total of 16 movements for 6 seconds each *(approximately 3 minute dynamic warm-up stretching sequence).*

1
2
5

3
4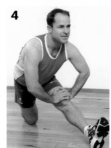
6

7
8

1. Start by performing 6 x stationary lunges with left leg forward.
2. Lower rear knee to ground and tilt pelvis forward to stretch rear thigh for 6 seconds.
3. Lower left forearm onto front thigh whilst extending right arm overhead and leaning the body across to the left side for 6 seconds.
4. Lean body back and straighten front leg whilst placing hands on thigh to support lower back and stretch for 6 seconds.
5. Bend the front leg and rest across shin whilst taking rear leg across body and resting on forearms and stretching for 6 seconds.
6. Raise onto both hands in a front support position and rest the right foot on the heel of the left foot and stretch for 3 seconds before performing a few light bounces for 3 seconds.
7. Step the left leg forwards and place both hands on front thigh keeping torso long and tall whilst stretching for 6 seconds.
8. Step forward with feet shoulder-width apart, with arms inside knee whilst pushing knees out for 6 second stretch.

Coach Collins™ Warm-up Sequence Cycle 2

Using a light pair of dumbbells, perform the following exercise sequence in a continuous manner. Perform eight (8) repetitions before moving onto the next exercise – without rest! This aims in warming up the muscles, tendons and joints of the upper body for more demanding exercises ahead as well as bringing focus and attention to establishing good body position. Hence, any muscular tension or restriction at this stage needs to be addressed prior to further training.

1. Perform 8 x front raises
2. Perform 8 x side raises
3. Perform 8 x upright rows
4. Perform 8 x bent over rows
5. Perform 8 x overhead presses
6. Perform 8 x biceps curls
7. Perform 8 x triceps extensions
8. Perform 8 x 45-degree chest presses

Coach Collins™ Warm-up Sequence Cycle 3

Using a light pair of dumbbells, perform the following exercise sequence in a continuous manner. Perform eight (8) repetitions before moving onto the next exercise – without rest! This aims in warming up the muscles, tendons and joints of the lower body.

1. Perform 8 x alternate leg lunges
2. Perform 8 x overhead squats
3. Perform 8 x alternate leg side lunges
4. Perform 8 x push-presses

The next stage of a dumbbell warm-up involves performing one set of repetitions using a lighter pair of dumbbells prior to each specific strength exercise. This enables you bring focus and attention to each exercise and the more demanding dumbbell weight that soon follows.

Progressive Resistance Training

In any physical activity, your muscles grow in response to the challenge placed upon them. Over time the muscles adapt to this stimulus and require an additional challenge for muscular strength gains to occur. The stimulus for this to occur evolves around **'8 Key Elements'**, some of which work simultaneously together, including:

8 Key Elements	Description
1. Exercise intensity	Weight (or mass) being lifted; based upon a percentage of one's maximum lift or 1RM (repetition maximum) used by advanced athletes and coaches for establishing training loads, reps and sets
2. Speed of movement – repetition ratio	Speed ratio of concentric and eccentric movement as well as mass being lifted – i.e. slow, fast or a combination of both, for example - 3:1:1 Ratio (or 3 seconds eccentric, 1 second transition, 1 second concentric) used in hypertrophy. Variations of these ratios apply, which can manipulate the intensity and max-strength gains
3. Time muscle is under tension	Number of repetitions being performed; speed of movement and the exercise intensity
4. Type of exercise	Actual exercise and movement being performed for specific muscle group – as there are many variations for each muscle group
5. Volume of work	Total number of repetitions and sets being performed as well as the frequency
6. Rest periods	Recovery period between exercises and sets can dictate fatigue or regeneration
7. Frequency	How often you train each week
8. Mental focus	How much effort and focus you put into your training session

In strength training using dumbbells, variations of these '8 Key Elements' play a major role in the outcome of your training. Many people can lift weights for years without change to their body shape or strength levels. So, to help take you to a new level in your training knowledge, understanding and approach we utilize the **Foundation Strength Training Zone Chart** (as follows). This training guideline is aimed at helping you understand the training zone you need to work on in order to improve your strength and your goals. Along the journey, there is a little work to be done by regularly adapting and applying the **8 Key Elements** as part of the Foundation Strength Training Zones.

Foundation Strength Training Zones	Repetition Range	Percentage of 1RM	Training effect
1. **Muscle Endurance** • **Stages 1-2**	12-20+ reps	40-60%	Aimed at developing a muscle's ability to contract over an extended period. Primarily for use in Stages 1 and 2 to allow the muscles, tendons and joints of the body time to adapt as part of a general preparation phase all athletes must acquire.
2. **Muscle Hypertrophy** • **Stage 1**	8-12 reps	60-80%	Aimed at solely increasing the cross-sectional area of the targeted muscle. In many instances, better results come from a slower speed of movement ratio for each repetition. Primarily for use in Stage 1.
3. **Maximal Strength** **Testing RM** (repetition maximum) • **Stages 1 & 3**	4-8 reps 1-3 reps	80-90% 100%	Aimed at increasing one's neuromuscular efficiency, strength and coordination between muscle groups. In many instances, better results come from a faster speed of movement without technique breakdown. Primarily for use in Stages 1 and 3 and also used for testing one's 1-3RM for assessment and measuring improvements.
4. **Power** **(a) Technique** – can be applied with stages 1-3 in order to obtain skill and lifting technique **(b) Explosive movements** • **Stage 3**	4-8 reps 1-5 reps	30-60% 75-100%	Aimed at transferring maximal strength gains by increasing the speed at which you apply a force using more complex exercises such as multi-joint and Olympic-Lifting techniques using dumbbells. Technique needs to first be learned at a lower intensity before applying more explosive force using heavier dumbbells. Primarily for use in Stage 3.

Outcome: Each strength-training zone targets the two specific skeletal muscle tissue fibers in different ways. Consisting of both **slow twitch** (aerobic-orientated) and **fast twitch** (anaerobic) contracting muscle fibers, the speed and intensity at which you train manipulates how the muscles respond and work together. As muscle fibers blend together, the slow twitch element responds generally to low power production and resistance to fatigue; whereas fast twitch fibers, which have low fatigue resistance, respond to high power production important in power sports and sprinting. This helps dictate the training cycles you undertake in order to build a strength foundation towards a more powerful foundation using a periodization model.

In most instances, no single training model fits all. So, think of this chart like a tree without branches. What I'm providing you with here is a training model that provides a benchmark for you to apply, but as you grow so do your branches (just like that of a tree) and variables of the strength training zones need to be adjusted, adapted and manipulated from the '8 Key Elements'. For instance, a simple adjustment of the speed of movement can make dramatic changes to the training intensity. A common mistake often made by athletes and gym-goers is moving the dumbbell or performing an exercise too fast. Here's one example:

If your goal is to build your chest region and you were performing 8 reps in 8 seconds (1 second a rep) on the dumbbell bench press, the time the muscle is under tension is minimal compared to if I asked you to perform each repetition using a 3:1:1 ratio – 3 seconds lowering, 1 second transition/hold and 1 second explosion upwards with dumbbells (for a 5 second repetition x 8 reps = 45 seconds under tension). Whilst strength gains may occur performing faster repetitions, increasing the cross-sectional area or size of a muscle works best following the 3:1:1 ratio – or its variations such as 3:0:1 or 2:0:1. In saying this, a faster speed (and heavier dumbbells) may be used at certain times within a training plan to increase maximum-strength – to suit your training objectives. There is where our training process called periodization fits into the equation incorporating the 8 Key Elements, Foundation Strength Training Zone's and the information that follows.

Periodization Plan

To help maximize one's performance all-year-round, we transfer the foundation training zone chart phases into a scheduled training cycle called periodization. This process allows an athlete to plan yearly, quarterly, monthly, weekly and even daily the type of training they will perform in order to work towards peaking for an event or series of events. Within this framework, training loads and volumes (sets, reps, percentage of maximum lifts) are manipulated in order to achieve specific training goals.

The scientific nature of this training approach relates to the specific requirements of each sport. For a seasonal athlete, a training cycle may consist of a 12-month period involving an off-season (transition) phase, pre-season and competition phases. This annual training plan is subdivided into periods of time to suit these phases for improving strength or fitness or speed over a period of time. This is referred to as macro-cycles, for example, a preparatory phase may consist of 16-weeks; within this 16-week period it may be broken down into 4 x 4-week cycles (macro-cycles) that build up in intensity towards the competition phase. Within a macro-cycle are smaller weekly cycles called micro-cycles that are used to plan daily training sessions.

The benefit of a periodization plan is that it provides a training plan platform for improvements in strength, maximum strength and power to occur through ongoing measurement testing. In a sporting environment where multiple physical components such as speed, fitness, strength and agility and skills sessions are required in parallel the periodization plan allows you to plan each session as well as recovery. Think of it like attending school or college where you have a yearly class schedule broken down into terms or semesters with holiday breaks in-between. Along the way there is regular testing just like playing competitive sport before a final series (or final exam).

Here is a general example of how a periodization plan for a sporting team may look – with multiple variations for each sport:

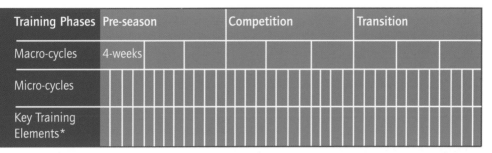

Training Phases	Pre-season			Competition			Transition		
Macro-cycles	4-weeks								
Micro-cycles									
Key Training Elements*									

Within each macro-cycle (4 weeks) is a weekly micro-cycle involving key training elements* such as: Strength, Speed, Agility, VO_2-Max, Testing and so forth along with skills training that accommodate the sports-specific requirements. In the case of Dynamic Dumbbell Training you could incorporate a periodization plan with a specific goal of improving strength, muscle size or fat loss – through measurable targets and testing and training applying a linear or non-linear training approach.

Linear and Non-Linear Training Approach

In Dynamic Dumbbell Training, we start off with a **linear training approach** which involves establishing a strength foundation (training base), improving technique and muscle fiber response whilst working towards maximal power output in stage 3. The linear training approach involves decreasing the volume and increasing the intensity each week in order to maximize strength, power or combination of both. There are many variables that can be used (refer back to 8 Key Elements). Here is one example:

• Weeks 1-4:   1 x 12-15reps
• Weeks 5-8:   2 x 10-12reps
• Weeks 9-12:   3 x 8-10reps
• Weeks 13-16: 4 x 6-8reps

A **non-linear approach** alternating between phases of higher volume and higher intensity throughout a cycle can also be applied for more advanced athletes and those within a competitive period. For instance, a non-linear approach may be performed over 3-4-week cycles or within a weekly cycle itself, for example: Monday low intensity (12-15 reps); Wednesday high intensity (6-8 reps) and Friday moderate intensity (10-12) reps. Below are three periodization cycle samples combining the above approaches into 8 16-week training cycles:

(1)   12-week periodization model for the beginner

(2)   12-week periodization model for the intermediate and more advanced

(3)   8-week advanced training cycle

Note: With multiple training variables existing, the following samples provide a baseline training approach for you to build a greater knowledge, awareness and understanding of training cycles and how your body responds. You may find some athletes, trainers or coaches may criticize or be negative towards such cycles, but just remember everyone has a starting point, even themselves, from which they will have once progressed and built upon – just like these. So, once you have hands-on experience in the gym and have successfully worked through these cycles and periodization plan together with future progression through Stages 1-3 incorporating the 8 Key Elements and Foundation Strength Training Zone's within this book, you too can make specific adaptions and modifications to your training program with an approach that best suits your specific body type and training needs.

12-Week Beginner's Cycle

This cycle is designed for the beginner, gym–enthusiast or athlete returning to training after a lengthy lay-off – as the first 4 weeks are important in preparing the muscles, tendons and joints for the training cycles ahead and reducing the risk of injury. This general model is broken down into 4-week progressive cycles. After 4 weeks' initial training, the percentage of 1RM is established under the guidance of a professional strength and conditioning coach and used as a guideline throughout each 4-week cycle, namely weeks 5 and 12, where it is re-tested. A recovery period (or lighter week of loading) may also be included every 4th week or between cycles.

Weeks 1-4	Muscle Endurance utilizing exercises from Stage 1.
Weeks 5-8	Muscle Hypertrophy utilizing exercises from Stage 1.
Weeks 9-12	Maximum Strength utilizing exercises from Stage 1 whilst also introducing more technical drills from Stage 2 and 3 using light dumbbells for learning good technique.

12-Week Intermediate to Advanced Cycle

In this cycle, an intermediate to advanced level athlete or trainer will have already established a sound training base for the support structures and starts with hypertrophy approach in weeks 1-4 before progressing. A recovery period (or lighter week of loading) may also be included every 4th week or between cycles.

Weeks 1-4	Muscle hypertrophy utilizing exercises from Stage 1.
Weeks 5-8	Maximum strength utilizing exercises from Stage 1 and 2.
Weeks 9-12	Power conversion utilizing exercises from Stages 1-3.

8-Week Advanced Strength/Power Training Cycle

In this cycle, an advanced trainer or athlete can apply rotating cycles of high and medium intensity exercise over 3 weeks followed by a light CNS (Central Nervous System) week before transitioning into a new 4-week training cycle. The objective is focused on in-season training cycles for the advanced athlete that can be modified to suit their training or competition schedule accordingly as well as a maintenance period.

Weeks 1-4	Maximum strength utilizing exercises from Stages 1-3.
Weeks 5-8	Power conversion utilizing exercises from Stage 3.
Weeks 9+	Maintenance of power.

Training Notes

The initiative throughout each 4-week training cycle is to gradually increase the volume (sets, reps and frequency) and intensity (described here as a percentage of your 1-Repetition Maximum – 1RM) to allow you to work towards a peak level. In some instances you may extend the cycle by an extra week or two also by applying a low, medium and high intensity schedule (non-linear approach).

Rest and recovery also plays a significant role during each training cycle with many athletes performing a light week of training during the final week of each phase as a transition into the next one. Appropriate rest and recovery is also important for growth, development and ongoing strength and muscle improvements throughout each training week – allowing muscle fibers and energy systems to adapt and recover to avoid overtraining and possible overuse injury.

It is also recommended to work with a professional strength and conditioning coach in the proper development of a periodization plan designed specifically for your training needs or athletic pursuit.

Repetition Maximum (RM) Testing – 1RM to 5RM

Intensity in exercise is most easily represented as a percentage of one's maximum lift. Establishing this maximal percentage is important in the overall training model as it provides a benchmark from which your training loads and repetitions are based. One of the most universally accepted methods for testing strength and power is the 1RM or the maximum amount of weight the athlete can lift for no more than one complete repetition of that strength related exercise. This method allows you to determine the loads used throughout the training program and is generally only applied to compound (multi-joint) exercises such as: Bench Press, Squat or Power Clean.

A minimum 4-8 week training base is required prior to attempting any repetition maximum tests to ensure the muscle, joints and tendons have adapted and proper technique has been established. This test should only be performed under the guidance of a professional strength and conditioning coach or personal trainer for accuracy and safety reasons. Most importantly, this can be re-tested throughout the training cycle as a tool that allows one to gauge whether to increase or decrease one's training load.

Now before I go any further I'd like you to recognize that performing a 1RM attempt is not the preferred method for a novice, but an intermediate or advanced lifter, because of the high intensity and risk level. Instead, working with a weight that can be lifted for 5 repetitions (5RM) which equates to approximately 87.5% of your maximum from which a 1RM can be calculated, is the preferred method for a novice.

Testing Method

To begin, start with a cardiovascular warm-up and light stretch. This is followed by a warm-up set of 12 repetitions of the specific exercise to be tested using a light weight. Rest for 60 seconds whilst increasing the weight to perform 8 repetitions followed by a 120-second rest. With your strength and conditioning coach, estimate what you believe your 5 repetition maximum weight will be. This means that you can only just complete a 5th rep and not 6 reps. If attempting the 5RM and you only complete 3 reps or so, rest for 180 seconds before attempting with a lighter weight.

Dumbbell Bench Press 5RM Example: (after initial cardiovascular warm-up)

1. Dumbbell bench press warm-up exercise performing 12 reps using light dumbbells.
2. Rest 60 seconds.
3. Dumbbell bench press warm-up exercise performing 8 reps of medium weight.
4. Rest 120 seconds.
5. Dumbbell bench press with estimated 5RM weighted dumbbells (always have a spotter or trainer on hand to assist with test).
6. If too easy or too heavy and more or less repetitions are completed, rest for 180 seconds before repeating this test with new estimated weight.
7. Once correct, multiply the 5RM (as 87.5% of your 1RM) as shown in the calculation below:

Example 5RM lift:
Pair of 40kg dumbbells (80kg total or 176lbs) into a 1RM outcome:

$$\frac{100 \times \text{weight lifted}}{87.5} = \frac{100 \times 80kg}{87.5} = 91.4kg \text{ (rounded off to 90kg)}$$

Once a 1RM can be established, training loads for various repetitions and total volume in training can also be established.

Note: The smallest weight increments in heavy lifts often equate to 5lbs (or 2.2kg) per dumbbell. If whilst performing a 5RM, only 4.5 reps are completed, you could generally announce that a reduction of 5kg off the total weight you could perform for 5 reps. Always round off your total score to a zero (0) or 5 number (i.e. 100kg or 105kg or 220lbs and so forth). Note: 1 kilogram (kg) = 2.2 pounds (lbs).

Estimating Training Loads							
1 rep	2 reps	3 reps	4 reps	6 reps	8 reps	10 reps	12 reps
100%	95%	92.5%	90%	85%	80%	75%	65%

For an advanced trainer or elite athlete, the 1RM-specific test may be performed using a similar example as above with lighter weights and higher reps followed by recovery period before increasing weight and reducing the reps near maximal loads.

Quite often when you transfer a 1RM score into a workout schedule (i.e. 3 sets of 12 reps at 65% of 1RM) you may find that you are able to perform 1 or 2 sets easy and unable to complete the third. This is when you know you are on the right track, because as your strength and muscle endurance improves and you are able to complete 3 sets easily, then the weight being lifted must be increased. On the other hand, if 65% is initially too hard this may need to be reduced to what your body tells you (i.e. 55-60%). Remember, these tables only act as a guideline from which you can adapt your training model. The **8 Key Elements** must also be taken into consideration as well as the specific **Foundation Strength Training Zones** as some exercises may be performed slower (time under tension) or faster than others.

Dynamic Dumbbell Training Guidelines – A Few Rules!

Prior to commencing any dumbbell or weights training program, there are a few guidelines you'll need to adhere to:

- Always gain approval to exercise by your doctor and physical therapist.
- If you have any prior or current lower back, quadratus lumborum, hip or gluteal muscular tension or a previous injury to these or surrounding areas, you are advised to work with your physical therapist and doctor prior to performing any of the following exercises to gain approval and ensure free range of movement without any stress.
- It is important during this phase that a proper warm-up, cool down and stretching routine is adapted to ensure effective range of motion is maintained and improved.
- Stretching is recommended before, during and after exercise, unless a joint or series of joints are hypermobile and require a stability approach. Stretches are short (6 seconds) in nature before and during exercise with a major focus on stretches being held for longer periods (15-30 seconds or more) after training.
- Each exercise should be preceded by a warm-up set using a light resistance (50%) for the specific exercise that follows.
- Apply 3B's Principle™ - Brace, Breath and Body Position with each exercise.
- Always maintain good posture and body alignment by focusing on the exercise at hand.
- Maintain deep breathing throughout each exercise. Breathe in on recovery and breathe out when exerting a force.
- Never sacrifice your lifting technique for a heavier weight.
- Always train under the guidance of certified strength and conditioning coach, Olympic Lifting coach or personal trainer.
- Use a spotter/trainer to help with each exercise as required.
- Always cool down and stretch after lifting.

In the following chapter you will find exercises used to strengthen each muscular region of the body.

CHAPTER 3

STAGE 1: STRENGTH

Strength Training is a key component for success in many sports and physical activities. In Stage 1, the objective is to develop a solid foundation of strength and strength endurance by focusing on enhancing one's muscular framework through a progressive overload using dumbbells for all muscle groups.

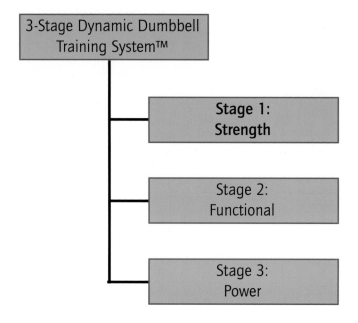

3-Stage Dynamic Dumbbell Training System™

Stage 1: Strength

Stage 2: Functional

Stage 3: Power

This chapter focuses on key exercises for improving muscular gains throughout the body. Exercises include both isolated single joint and compound multi-joint exercises in the following muscle regions:

- **Abs & Core**
- **Arms**
  - Biceps
  - Triceps
- **Back**
- **Chest**
- **Legs**
  - Deadlifts
  - Lunges
  - Squats
  - Calves
- **Shoulders**

Abs & Core

The abdominal and lower back muscles combine to form the core region of the body. The core region helps stabilize the body for more efficient and effective movement patterns to occur between the upper and lower body. Exercises that target the Rectus abdominus and obliques through various angles and intensities as well as the lower back and deeper transversus abdominis muscle. In addition, a number of compound exercises such as squats also strengthen the abdominal (torso) region.

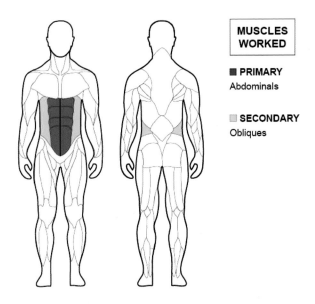

MUSCLES WORKED

■ **PRIMARY**
Abdominals

▨ **SECONDARY**
Obliques

Rectus Abdominis
- Flexes the trunk

Obliques
- Rotate, flex, side bend the trunk. Support viscera and assist exhalation.

Iliopsoas
- Flexes hip.

Lower Back Muscles
- Extend the spine backwards, some side bend and spinal rotation.

Abdominal exercises are often progressed through a series of core-isometric bracing and breathing drills to build static postural endurance. This is then followed by a series of muscular contraction exercises involving the abdominals and obliques as well as Iliopsoas, quadratus lumborum (sideways movement) and lower back region, collectively referred to as the core or torso region.

Single Leg Dish Hold

Start   Raised

Instruction

- Lie on your back in an extended position with one leg bent, the other straight and arms extended overhead gripping a single dumbbell – arms pressed against ears.

- Apply 3B's Principle™ - Brace, Breath and Body Position.

- Simultaneously raise arms and shoulders and one leg into body dish (banana shape) position and hold.

- Keep body long and extended ensuring the abdominals are activated and lower back remains in contact with the floor at all times and toe of raised leg is pointed. If not, stop the exercise immediately and lower.

- Hold this position for a short period of time (i.e. 5-15 seconds or more) using an isometric hold approach or raising up for 2 seconds then lowering for 2 seconds to complete one repetition.

- Maintain neutral head and neck alignment with body at all times.

- Lower and repeat with opposite leg bent.

Body Dish

Start   Raised

Instruction

- Lie on your back in an extended position with one leg bent, the other straight and arms extended overhead gripping a single dumbbell – arms pressed against ears.
- Apply 3B's Principle™ - Brace, Breath and Body Position.
- Simultaneously raise arms and legs into body dish (banana shape) position and hold.
- Keep body long and extended ensuring the abdominals are activated and lower back remains in contact with the floor at all times and toe of raised leg is pointed. If not, stop the exercise immediately and lower.
- Hold this position for a short period of time (i.e. 5-15 seconds or more) using an isometric hold approach or raising up for 2 seconds then lowering for 2 seconds to complete one repetition.
- Maintain neutral head and neck alignment with body at all times.

Toe Touch

Start

Raised

Instruction

- Lie on your back with legs raised from hip at 90 degrees and slightly bent and arms extended up above eye line gripping a single dumbbell in both hands at either end.
- Apply 3B's Principle™ - Brace, Breath and Body Position.
- Breathing out, raise shoulders off the ground and reach dumbbell up towards feet.
- Breathe in and lower.
- Avoid swinging legs or taking hip angle beyond 90 degrees due to the stress placed on the lower back region.
- Aim to raise for 2 seconds and lower for 2 seconds to complete one repetition – for good muscle contraction.

Overhead Toe Touch

Start   Raised

Instruction

- Lie on your back with legs raised from hip at 90 degrees and slightly bent and arms extended overhead on the ground gripping a single dumbbell in both hands at either end.
- Apply 3B's Principle™ - Brace, Breath and Body Position.
- Breathing out, simultaneously raise dumbbell, arms and shoulders off the ground by contracting the abdominal region.
- Breathe in and lower.
- Aim to raise for 2 seconds and lower for 2 seconds to complete one repetition – for good muscle contraction.

Abdominal Crunch Series: Levels 1–3

Level 1: Start   Raised

Level 2: Start   Raised

Level 3: Start   Raised

Instruction

- Lie on your back on ground with your knees bent and feet resting on the ground shoulder-width apart with the following arm positions:
  - Level 1 (easy – short lever): Arms across chest holding single dumbbell.
  - Level 2 (moderate – mid-lever): Arms bent; dumbbell resting against forehead.
  - Level 3 (hard – long lever): Arms extended overhead holding single dumbbell.
- Apply 3B's Principle™ - Brace, Breath and Body Position.
- Breathing out, contract the abdominal muscles and slowly contract and curl the stomach muscles up bringing the sternum towards the pelvis.
- Breathe in and lower.
- Maintain the head in its neutral position throughout to avoid neck tension.
- Aim to curl and raise up for 2 seconds and lower for 2 seconds to complete one repetition.

Fitness Ball Crunch Series: Levels 1–3

Level 1: Start · Raised

Level 2: Start · Raised

Level 3: Start · Raised

Instruction

- Lie on your back on Fitness Ball with your knees bent and feet resting on the ground shoulder-width apart with the following arm positions:
    - Level 1 (easy – short lever): Arms across chest holding single dumbbell.
    - Level 2 (moderate – mid-lever): Arms bent; dumbbell resting against forehead.
    - Level 3 (hard – long lever): Arms extended overhead holding single dumbbell.
- Apply 3B's Principle™ - Brace, Breath and Body Position.
- Breathing out, contract the abdominal muscles and slowly contract and curl the stomach muscles up bringing the sternum towards the pelvis.
- Breathe in and lower.
- Maintain the head in its neutral position throughout to avoid neck tension.
- Aim to curl and raise up for 2 seconds and lower for 2 seconds to complete one repetition.

Collins-Lateral Fly™

Start   Raised

Instruction

- Lie on side with upper body supported by the elbow (90 degrees, directly below shoulder), forearm and clenched fist. Lower body supported by feet – positioned together along with legs – resting on edge of shoe.
- The upper arm is bent holding dumbbell in front of body across chest area and close to supporting hand on the ground.
- Lift the pelvis off the ground, eliminating the side bending by raising onto the edge of shoes, forming a straight line from the feet to head.
- Apply 3B's Principle™ - Brace, Breath and Body Position.
- Maintaining a deep breathing pattern, raise the upper arm in a semi-circular motion until vertical then lower to complete one repetition.
- Raise upper leg to increase the challenge whilst lowering and raising arm.
- Repeat drill raising opposite arm whilst resting on opposite forearm.
- Raise upper leg to add intensity to the movement through core control.

Lateral Side Raises

Start   Raised

Instruction

- Lie on your side, legs extended, toes pointed and feet together.
- The arm closest to the ground extends above head with palm facing up towards ceiling holding a dumbbell – head relaxed resting on inner part of arm.
- The upper arm is bent, supporting your body weight in front of the body.
- Apply 3B's Principle™ - Brace, Breath and Body Position.
- Maintaining a long body position and deep breathing pattern, simultaneously raise legs and arm with dumbbell into the air, then lower to complete one repetition.
- Start slow and increase speed of motion – maintaining control and coordination at all times.
- Maintain tight and long body position by leaning body slightly forward and putting weight onto hand supporting the body. Avoid leaning or falling backwards.
- Repeat lying on opposite side.

Elbow to Knee

Start   Raised

Instruction

- Lie on your back with one leg bent and the other foot resting on the opposite knee.
- Rest dumbbell on opposite shoulder to raised knee.
- Apply 3B's Principle™ - Brace, Breath and Body Position.
- Breathing out, raise opposite elbow across towards opposite knee.
- Breathe in and lower.
- Aim to raise dumbbell across for 2 seconds and lower for 2 seconds to complete one repetition – for good muscle contraction.
- Repeat on opposite side.

Variation: Extend bent leg and hold off ground – bringing knee in towards chest as elbow raises and cross to opposite side; then extending back out again.

Single Arm Toe Touch

Start   Midpoint

Instruction

- Lie on your back with legs raised vertically from hip at 90 degrees and slightly bent.
- Extend left arm vertically holding dumbbell whilst the right arm is resting by your side on the ground.
- Apply 3B's Principle™ - Brace, Breath and Body Position.
- Breathing out, raise left shoulder off the ground reaching hand towards foot.
- Breathe in and lower.
- Aim to raise dumbbell up for 2 seconds and lower for 2 seconds to complete one repetition – for good muscle contraction.
- Repeat with right arm.

Dumbbell Isometric Twist

Start   Rotate

Instruction

- Sit on ground with body at approximately a 45-degree angle with legs extended and slightly bent and arms extended forwards holding a single one dumbbell in both hands – at either end.

- Apply 3B's Principle™ - Brace, Breath and Body Position.

- Maintaining a constant breathing pattern, with the abdominals braced and shoulders square, move the dumbbell from side to side – just outside the line of knee – using the arms only – in a controlled manner for a set amount of time or repetitions.

- This movement uses primarily the arms and limits any body rotation or lower back twisting to avoid overuse or stress.

Fitness Ball Seated Twist

Start   Rotate

Instruction

- Sit on ground with fitness ball resting against upper back – positioned on floor against wall – with body at approximately 45-degree angle; legs extended and slightly bent and arms also extended forwards holding a single one dumbbell in both hands – at either end.

- Apply 3B's Principle™ - Brace, Breath and Body Position.

- Maintaining a constant breathing pattern, move the dumbbell from side to side, just outside the line of knee whilst rotating the shoulders and body across the fitness ball for support in a controlled manner for a set amount of time or repetitions.

- The use of the fitness ball helps reduce the load on the lower back – adjust body position accordingly to ensure good posture and muscle activation.

Fitness Ball Oblique Twist

Start   Midpoint

Instruction

- Lie on ball at shoulder height with hips raised and body parallel to ground with feet shoulder-width apart, arms extended above chest holding one dumbbell in both hands – at either end.
- Apply 3B's Principle™ - Brace, Breath and Body Position.
- Keep the arms in-line with the upper body, slowly twist the arms and shoulders across to the left side – simultaneously bending at the knee and rotating the hip and torso with left shoulder rising onto ball and arms parallel to ground.
- Keeping arms extended, rotate the dumbbell across the body to the right side up onto the right shoulder with arms once again parallel to the ground.
- Move head in time with body and in line with shoulder in neutral position. Twist slowly under tension for 3 seconds to each side.

Reverse Curls

Start   Midpoint

Instruction

- Lie flat on your back with your knees bent, feet on ground and arms by your side, resting dumbbell between your legs at thigh level.
- Apply 3B's Principle™ - Brace, Breath and Body Position.
- Maintaining a deep breathing pattern, simultaneously draw the lower abdominal muscles in and raise legs up together until buttocks lift off ground and thighs reach vertical, before slowly lowering legs and feet back to ground to complete one repetition.
- Increase lift action from pelvic region once abdominal muscles become stronger whilst ensuring the head, neck and shoulders remain relaxed.

Dumbbell Front Raise

Start   Midpoint

Instruction

- Stand in semi-squat position with feet shoulder width apart and arms extended down in front of body gripping a single dumbbell, held vertically, in both hands at waist height.
- Apply 3B's Principle™ - Brace, Breath and Body Position.
- Breathe out as you simultaneously raise the dumbbell up in a semi-circular motion in front of body up to eye level whilst straightening both legs.
- Breathe in as you reverse the movement – simultaneously lowering arms back down the waist height whilst legs lowering into semi-squat position to complete one repetition.
- Ensure abdominals remain braced at all times to limit any stress on the lower back region.

A deeper squat can also be performed using a larger wood chopping movement of the arms. This exercise challenges the core abdominal brace through an arm raising and lowering motion which also helps strengthen the shoulders.

Dumbbell Side Bend

Start

Midpoint

Instruction
- Stand tall with feet hip-width apart and both arms extended down by side with one gripping a dumbbell – knuckles facing outwards.
- Apply 3B's Principle™ - Brace, Breath and Body Position.
- Bend sideways at waist and slowly lower dumbbell down towards lateral side of knee – without any forward or backward movement.
- Reverse movement raising back up and across to the opposite side to complete one repetition.
- Repeat movement with dumbbell in opposite hand.

Weighted Side Bends

Start   Raised

Instruction

- Lie on side on fitness ball with top leg backwards and lower leg forwards, for good base support, whilst holding a single dumbbell in lower hand against side of head and upper hand resting on waist.
- Apply 3B's Principle™ - Brace, Breath and Body Position.
- Raise side of torso up by lateral flexion upwards from the waistline.
- Lower torso back down on ball to complete one repetition.
- Repeat movement on opposite side.

Tick Tocks

Start   Midpoint

Instruction

- Stand tall with feet hip-width apart and both arms extended above head gripping a single a dumbbell in both hands at either end – knuckles facing outwards.
- Apply 3B's Principle™ - Brace, Breath and Body Position.
- Keeping torso long, bend sideways at the waist and slowly lower dumbbell 15-30 degrees to the right side in a controlled motion– without any forward or backward movement.
- Reverse movement bending sideways across to the left side to complete one repetition.

100 Drill

Starting Position   Midpoint

Instruction

- Lie on your back with legs raised together at approximately a 60-degree angle in an extended position – toes pointed – both arms raised parallel to the ground holding a light pair of dumbbells – palms facing downwards.

- Apply 3B's Principle™ - Brace, Breath and Body Position.

- Breathe out as you curl upper body and raise head – ribs drawn to the hips and navel drawn to the spine.

- Inhale for 5 arm pumps, up and down and exhale 5 pumps until you have reached 100 pumps or 10 breath cycles.

Hip Raise

Start   Midpoint

Instruction

- To help strengthen the lower back, lie flat on back on ground with legs bent and arms extended down at waist height with hands gripping a single dumbbell at both ends – knuckles facing outwards.
- Apply 3B's Principle™ - Brace, Breath and Body Position.
- Breathe in deeply.
- Breathe out and slowly peel the lower back off the ground and raise hips into the air.
- Breathe in at the top of the movement and re-activate abdominal muscles. Complete one full breath in and out – then in again before lowering body.
- Breathe out and lower the body in reverse motion lowering hips to ground.
- Maintain square hips at all times.

Variation: Balance on heels to introduce hamstrings muscle involvement.

Fitness Ball Extensions

Start   Midpoint

Instruction

- Lie on fitness ball on stomach and upper thighs, with feet shoulder-width apart on ground – resting single dumbbell in both hands at either end and resting on head.
- Apply 3B's Principle™ - Brace, Breath and Body Position.
- Keeping the body extended, raise the chest off the ball until a straight line is formed between the legs and upper body and then lower to complete one repetition.

ARMS
BICEPS

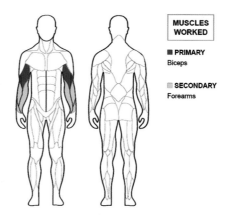

MUSCLES
WORKED

■ PRIMARY
Biceps

■ SECONDARY
Forearms

- **Biceps** – The front side of the upper arm which bend and supinate the elbow.
- **Forearms** – Collective muscles between the elbow and wrist bend the elbow, which pronate and supinate the elbow depending on the starting position.

Biceps Curl Variables

To assist with arm and body positioning in strengthening the biceps, the following table outlines variations on the biceps curl exercise used in this chapter.

Note: Reverse curl exercises to strengthen the forearm are included in this arm section.

Biceps Curls Variables				
Grip Variation	Palms forward – Open Curl	Hammer Grip – knuckles outwards	Hammer Grip with rotation	
Arm Movement	Both arms simultaneously	Single arm, alternate	Palms forward and up to shoulder	Hammer Grip position	Hammer Grip with rotation
Standing	Feet shoulder-width apart	Lunge Stance	Wall-sit position	Single leg	Kneeling
Seated	Flat Bench	Fitness Ball	Incline Bench – prone or supine	Preacher Bench	
Modified	Preacher Curl – both arms simultaneously	Preacher Curl – single arm	Incline Bench Single Arm	Fitness Ball Preacher Curl	Reverse grip chin-ups

Open Curls

| Start | Midpoint |

Instruction

- Stand tall with feet shoulder-width apart and arms extended down resting dumbbells by your side with palms facing forwards and upper arms held in close to your body at all times.
- Apply the 3B's Principle™ - Brace, Breath and Body Position.
- Breathe out as you simultaneously bend your elbows and curl both dumbbells up to shoulder height – keeping your wrists straight at all times.
- Breathe in as you lower the dumbbells down outside your thighs to complete one repetition.

Note: This exercise can also be performed seated or in standing lunge stance positions using a single arm or both arms simultaneously.

Rotation Curls

Start   Midpoint

Instruction

- Stand tall with feet shoulder-width apart and arms extended down resting dumbbells by your side with knuckles facing outwards and upper arms held in close to your body at all times.
- Apply the 3B's Principle™ - Brace, Breath and Body Position.
- Breathe out as you simultaneously bend your elbows and curl and rotate palms of both hands gripping dumbbells up to shoulder height – keeping your wrists straight at all times.
- Breathe in as you lower and rotate dumbbells back down by your side to complete one repetition.

Note: This exercise can also be performed seated or in standing lunge stance positions using a single arm or both arms simultaneously.

Alternate Arm Rotation Curl

Start   Midpoint

Instruction

- Stand tall with feet shoulder-width apart and arms extended down resting dumbbells by your side with knuckles facing outwards and upper arms held in close to your body at all times.
- Apply the 3B's Principle™ - Brace, Breath and Body Position.
- Breathe out as you bend one arm and curl and rotate dumbbell up to shoulder height with palm rotating inwards – keeping your wrist straight at all times.
- Breathe in as you lower and rotate dumbbell back down by your side to complete one repetition.
- Repeat movement with opposite arm.

Note: This exercise can also be performed seated or in standing lunge stance positions using a single arm or both arms simultaneously.

Hammer Curls

Start   Midpoint

Instruction

- Stand tall with feet shoulder-width apart and arms extended down resting dumbbells by your side with knuckles facing outwards and upper arms in held close to your body at all times.
- Apply the 3B's Principle™ - Brace, Breath and Body Position.
- Breathe out as you simultaneously bend your elbows and raise both dumbbells up to shoulder height keeping the hands in the same starting position and your wrists straight at all times.
- Breathe in as you lower both arms back down by your side to complete one repetition.

Note: This exercise can also be performed seated or in standing lunge stance positions using a single arm or both arms simultaneously.

Alternate Arm Hammer Curl

Start   Midpoint

Instruction

- Stand tall with feet shoulder-width apart and arms extended down resting dumbbells by your side with knuckles facing outwards and upper arms in held close to your body at all times.
- Apply the 3B's Principle™ - Brace, Breath and Body Position.
- Breathe out as you bend one arm and curl dumbbell up to shoulder height keeping the hands in the same starting position and your wrists straight at all times.
- Breathe in as you lower this arm back down by your side to complete one repetition.
- Repeat movement with opposite arm.

Note: This exercise can also be performed seated or in standing lunge stance positions using a single arm or both arms simultaneously.

Seated Curls

| Start | Midpoint |

Instruction

- Sit at end of flat weight bench with feet shoulder-width apart and arms extended down resting dumbbells by your side with palms facing forwards and upper arms held in close to your body at all times.
- Apply the 3B's Principle™ - Brace, Breath and Body Position.
- Breathe out as you simultaneously bend your elbows and curl both dumbbells up to shoulder height – keeping your wrists straight at all times.
- Breathe in as you lower the dumbbells down outside your thighs to complete one repetition.

Note: This exercise can also be performed seated on a Fitness Ball or 45-degree Incline Bench using a single arm or both arms simultaneously, placing variations across the muscle fibers.

Seated Hammer Curls

Start   Midpoint

Instruction

- Sit at end of flat weight bench with feet shoulder-width apart and arms extended down resting dumbbells by your side with knuckles facing outwards and upper arms in held close to your body at all times.
- Apply the 3B's Principle™ - Brace, Breath and Body Position.
- Breathe out as you simultaneously bend your elbows and raise both dumbbells up to shoulder height keeping the hands in the same starting position and your wrists straight at all times.
- Breathe in as you lower both arms back down by your side to complete one repetition.

Note: This exercise can also be performed seated on a Fitness Ball or 45-degree Incline Bench using a single arm or both arms simultaneously, placing variations across the muscle fibers.

Seated Alternate Arm Curl

Start   Midpoint

Instruction

- Sit at end of flat weight bench with feet shoulder-width apart and arms extended down resting dumbbells by your side with knuckles facing outwards and upper arms in held close to your body at all times
- Apply the 3B's Principle™ - Brace, Breath and Body Position
- Breathe out as you bend one arm and curl and rotate dumbbell up to shoulder height with palm rotating inwards – keeping your wrist straight at all times.
- Breathe in as you lower and rotate dumbbell back down by your side to complete one repetition.
- Repeat movement with opposite arm.

Note: This exercise can also be performed seated on a Fitness Ball or 45-degree Incline Bench using a single arm or both arms simultaneously, placing variations across the muscle fibers.

Fitness Ball Hammer Curls

Start   Midpoint

Instruction

- Sit on middle of Fitness Ball with feet shoulder-width apart and arms extended down resting dumbbells by your side with knuckles facing outwards and upper arms in held close to your body at all times.
- Apply the 3B's Principle™ - Brace, Breath and Body Position.
- Breathe out as you bend both arms simultaneously up to shoulder height – keeping your wrist straight and knuckles outwards at all times.
- Breathe in as you lower both dumbbells back down by your side to complete one repetition.

Note: This exercise can also be performed with a single arm – alternate arm raise.

Fitness Ball Rotation Curls

Start   Midpoint

Instruction

- Sit on middle of Fitness Ball with feet shoulder-width apart and arms extended down resting dumbbells by your side with knuckles facing outwards and upper arms in held close to your body at all times.
- Apply the 3B's Principle™ - Brace, Breath and Body Position.
- Breathe out as you bend both arms and curl and rotate dumbbell up to shoulder height with palm rotating inwards – keeping your wrist straight at all times.
- Breathe in as you lower and rotate dumbbell back down by your side to complete one repetition.

Note: This exercise can also be performed starting with an open palm grip and curling both arms up to shoulders as well as a single arm – alternate arm raise.

Fitness Ball Concentration Curl

Start   Midpoint

Instruction

- Sit on middle of Fitness Ball with feet shoulder-width apart and arms extended down resting dumbbells by your side with knuckles facing outwards and upper arms in held close to your body at all times.
- Apply the 3B's Principle™ - Brace, Breath and Body Position.
- Breathe out as you bend both arms and curl and rotate dumbbell up to shoulder height with palm rotating inwards – keeping your wrist straight at all times.
- Breathe in as you lower and rotate dumbbell back down by your side to complete one repetition.
- Repeat movement with opposite arm.

Note: This exercise can also be performed starting with an open palm grip and alternate arm raise.

Incline Bench Curls

Start   Midpoint

Instruction

- Sit on 45-degree incline bench with arms extended down by side of body with palms facing forwards.
- Apply the 3B's Principle™ - Brace, Breath and Body Position.
- Breathe out as you bend both arms and curl dumbbells up to shoulder height – knuckles forward.
- Ensure wrists are straight at all times and upper arm from shoulder to elbow vertical and close to body.
- Breathe in as you lower arms back down by your side to complete one repetition.

Note: This exercise can also be performed as a single arm alternate movement.

Incline Hammer Curls

Start   Midpoint

Instruction

- Sit on a 45-degree incline bench with arms extended down by side of body with palms facing inwards.
- Apply the 3B's Principle™ - Brace, Breath and Body Position.
- Breathe out as you bend both arms and curl dumbbells up to shoulder height – knuckles forward.
- Breathe out as you simultaneously bend your elbows and raise both dumbbells up to shoulder height keeping the hands in the same starting position and your wrists straight at all times.
- Ensure wrists are straight at all times and upper arm from shoulder to elbow vertical and close to body.
- Breathe in as you lower both arms back down by your side to complete one repetition.

Note: This exercise can also be performed with a single arm – alternate arm hammer grip raise.

Incline Alternate Concentration Curl

Start   Midpoint

Instruction
- Sit on a 45-degree incline bench with arms extended down by side of body with palms facing inwards with upper arms in held close to your body at all times.
- Apply the 3B's Principle™ - Brace, Breath and Body Position.
- Breathe out as you bend one arm and curl and rotate dumbbell up to shoulder height with palm rotating inwards – keeping your wrist straight at all times.
- Breathe in as you lower and rotate dumbbell back down by your side to complete one repetition.
- Repeat movement with opposite arm.

Note: This exercise can also be performed curling both arms up simultaneously.

Concentration Curls

Start   Midpoint

Instruction

- Sit on the end of a flat weight bench with feet and knees wider than shoulder-width apart.
- Gripping dumbbell in the right hand, lean forward and lower the elbow of the right arm on the inner side of the right thigh next to knee with knuckles facing in towards shin.
- Rest the left hand on the left thigh for support.
- Keeping your upper arm tucked into your thigh, breathe out as slowly curl the dumbbell up towards your right shoulder keeping wrist straight.
- Breathe in as you lower this arm back down to complete one repetition.
- Complete set and then repeat with opposite arm.

Variation: Use a Hammer Grip.

Preacher Bench Curls

Start   Midpoint

Instruction

- Sit on preacher curl bench with upper arms extended over pads – adjust accordingly – palms facing upwards.
- Apply the 3B's Principle™ - Brace, Breath and Body Position.
- Breathe out as you bend both arms and curl dumbbells up to shoulder height – knuckles forward.
- Ensure wrists are straight at all times and upper arm remains in contact with pad.
- Breathe in as you lower dumbbells back down to complete one repetition.

Preacher Curl Exercise Variations include:

- **Single Arm Alternate** – curling one arm at a time, then the other
- **Single Arm** – using one arm only
- **Hammer Grip** – raising both arms together with knuckles facing outwards
- **Single Arm Hammer Grip** – curling one arm at a time, then the other, with knuckles facing outwards
- **Hammer Grip Rotation** – start with hammer grip and rotate both arms up with palms facing shoulders
- **Hammer Grip Alternate Arm Rotation** – start with hammer grip and rotate one arm up with palm facing shoulders and back down, then the other
- **Single Arm Hammer Grip** – using one arm only
- **Single Arm Hammer Grip Arm Rotation** – using one arm only
- **Reverse Curls** – knuckles facing upwards to strengthen forearms

Fitness Ball Preacher Curls

Start   Midpoint

Instruction

- Kneel on ground and lie across fitness ball on stomach with arms extended forwards over ball with triceps muscle and elbow resting on ball and palms facing upwards.
- Apply the 3B's Principle™ - Brace, Breath and Body Position.
- Breathe out as you simultaneously bend your elbows and curl and rotate palms of both hands gripping dumbbells up to shoulder height – keeping your wrists straight at all times.
- Breathe in as you lower and rotate dumbbells back down by your side to complete one repetition.

Note: See Preacher Bench Curls variations on previous page for additional exercise variations.

Incline Bench Curls

Start   Midpoint

Instruction

- Stand behind an incline bench and extend arm over and down along bench with dumbbel in hand – palm facing upwards. Use opposite hand for support on bench.
- Apply the 3B's Principle™ - Brace, Breath and Body Position.
- Breathe out as you bend arm and curl dumbbell up to shoulder height – knuckles forward
- Ensure wrists are straight at all times and upper arm and elbow remains in contact with bench at all times.
- Breathe in as you lower the single dumbbell back down to complete one repetition.

Note: This exercise is a good option if no preacher curl bench is available and can also be performed using a hammer grip of reverse curl motion over a fitness ball.

Bench Curl Variations include:

- **Single Arm Hammer Grip** – curl one arm up with knuckles facing outwards.
- **Hammer Grip Rotation** – start with hammer grip position and rotate arm up with palm facing shoulders.
- **Reverse Curls** – knuckles facing upwards to strengthen forearms.

Wall Squat Curls

Start   Midpoint

Instructions
- To reduce any forward movement or assistance with dumbbell curls, apply the wall squats curl position.
- Lean back against wall with feet one step forward and slide down wall until your thighs are at approximately a 110-degree angle with arms extended down by your side with palms facing inwards.
- Apply the 3B's Principle™ - Brace, Breath and Body Position.
- Breathe out as you simultaneously bend your elbows and curl and rotate palms of both hands gripping dumbbells up to shoulder height – keeping your wrists straight at all times.
- Breathe in as you lower and rotate dumbbells back down by your side to complete one repetition.

Note: The wall sit position helps prevent any upper body swinging or cheating.
See pages 60-64 for arm exercise variations.

Reverse Curls

Start   Midpoint

Instruction

- Stand tall with your knees slightly bent and feet shoulder-width apart gripping dumbbells in both hands with an overhand grip – knuckles facing forwards – resting on thighs.
- Apply the 3B's Principle™ - Brace, Breath and Body Position.
- Breathe out as you bend your elbow and raise both dumbbells up to shoulder height – palms now facing forwards – and wrists remaining straight.
- Breathe in as you lower the dumbbells back down to your thighs to complete one repetition.

Note: This forearm exercise can be performed seated, kneeling or standing using a single arm or both arms simultaneously.

Seated Reverse Curls – Forearms

Start   Midpoint

Instruction

- Sit at end of flat weight bench with feet shoulder-width apart and arms extended down resting dumbbells by your side with knuckles facing forwards and upper arms in held close to your body at all times.
- Apply the 3B's Principle™ - Brace, Breath and Body Position.
- Breathe out as you bend your elbow and raise both dumbbells up to shoulder height – palms now facing forwards – and wrists remaining straight.
- Breathe in as you lower the dumbbells back down to your thighs to complete one repetition.

Note: This forearm exercise can also be performed standing, kneeling or seated on a Fitness Ball or 45-degree Incline Bench using a single arm or both arms simultaneously, placing variations across the muscle fibers of the forearms.

Seated Wrist Curl Extension

Start   Midpoint

Instruction

- Sit on the end of a flat weight bench with feet and knees wider than shoulder-width apart.
- Lean forward and lay your forearms on your upper thighs – knuckles facing upwards – with your wrists resting over your knees.
- Apply the 3B's Principle™ - Brace, Breath and Body Position.
- Lower dumbbells forwards of knees maintaining a tight grip.
- Curl dumbbells up as high as possible without raising your forearms to complete one repetition.

Note: This forearm exercise can be performed using a single hand or both hands simultaneously resting on the thighs or kneeling on ground with forearms resting over the edge of a flat weight bench. Avoid this exercise if you have any previous wrist or forearm stress, tension or injury.

Seated Wrist Curl Flexion

Start   Midpoint

Instruction
- Sit on the end of a flat weight bench with feet and knees wider than shoulder-width apart.
- Lean forward and lay your forearms on your upper thighs – palms facing upwards – with your wrists resting over your knees.
- Apply the 3B's Principle™ - Brace, Breath and Body Position.
- Lower dumbbells forwards of knees maintaining a tight grip.
- Curl dumbbells up as high as possible without raising your forearms to complete one repetition.

Note: This forearm exercise can be performed using a single hand or both hands simultaneously resting on the thighs or kneeling on ground with forearms resting over the edge of a flat weight bench. Avoid this exercise if you have any previous wrist or forearm stress, tension or injury.

TRICEPS

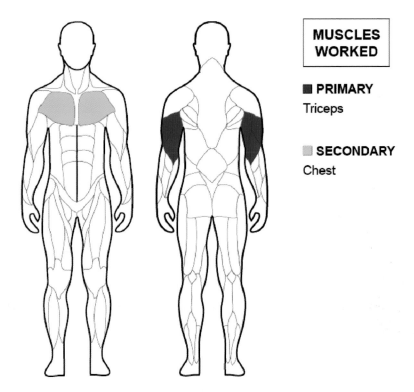

MUSCLES WORKED

■ **PRIMARY**
Triceps

■ **SECONDARY**
Chest

- **Triceps** – The rear side of the upper arm.
- **Pectoralis (Chest)** – Large fan-shaped muscle that covers the front of the upper chest.

Kneeling Kickback

Start   Midpoint

Instruction

- Stand next to flat weight bench.
- Kneel on bench with left knee and lean body forward resting left hand directly under shoulder on bench also with torso almost parallel to ground.
- Gripping dumbbell in right hand, raise upper arm close to the body until parallel to the ground; arm bent, knuckles facing downwards.
- Apply the 3B's Principle™ - Brace, Breath and Body Position.
- Breathe out as you extend left hand back and up until forearm is parallel to ground – wrist kept straight at all times.
- Breathe in as you lower the dumbbell back down, by bending the elbow, to complete one repetition.
- Repeat on opposite side.

Fitness Ball Kickback

Start | Midpoint

Instruction

- Lie on fitness ball on chest and stomach with feet shoulder-with apart on ground; upper arms held close to the body, elbows bent and hands gripping dumbbells with knuckles facing downwards.
- Apply the 3B's Principle™ - Brace, Breath and Body Position for good core control whilst lying on ball.
- Breathe out as you extend both hands back and up arm up until forearm is parallel to ground – wrist kept straight at all times and arms close to body.
- Breathe in as you lower the dumbbells back down, by bending the elbow, to complete one repetition.

Two-hand Bent Over Kickback

Start   Midpoint

Instruction

- Start in forward flexed position, with knees slightly bent, torso almost parallel to ground; upper arms held close to the body, elbows bent and hands gripping dumbbells with knuckles facing downwards.
- Apply the 3B's Principle™ - Brace, Breath and Body Position.
- Breathe out as you extend both hands back and up arm up until forearm is parallel to ground – wrist kept straight at all times and arms close to body.
- Breathe in as you lower the dumbbells back down, by bending the elbows, to complete one repetition.

Note: This exercise can also be performed with forehead resting on top of incline bench or torso 15 degrees above parallel.

Flat Bench Extensions

Start   Midpoint

Instruction
- Lie on back on flat weight bench with feet resting on ground for support shoulder width apart and both arms extended vertically and parallel gripping dumbbells – palms facing inwards.
- Apply the 3B's Principle™ - Brace, Breath and Body Position.
- Breathe in as you bend the elbows and lower both arms until forearms descend beyond parallel to the ground, either side of your head.
- Breathe out as you raise the dumbbells back up to the vertical starting position to complete one repetition.

Variation A: This exercise can also be performed on a 45-degree incline bench or fitness ball – resting on ball across upper back region.

Variation B: A single dumbbell can also be held gripping either end of dumbbell with elbows held close to the body and hands lowering down to forehead, bending at the elbows before raising and straightening arms.

Flat Bench Single Arm Extension

Start   Midpoint

Instruction

- Lie on back on flat weight bench with feet resting on ground for support shoulder-width apart and right arm extended vertically with the left arm gripping rear of left triceps for support.
- Apply the 3B's Principle™ - Brace, Breath and Body Position.
- Breathe in as you bend the left elbow and lower until forearm descends just past parallel to the ground.
- Breathe out as you raise the dumbbell back up to the vertical starting position to complete one repetition.
- Repeat with opposite arm.

Note: This exercise can also be performed on a 45-degree incline bench or fitness ball – resting on ball across upper back region.

Incline Extensions

Start   Midpoint

Instruction

- Lie on back on incline bench with feet resting on ground for support shoulder-width apart and both arms extended vertically and parallel gripping dumbbells – palms facing inwards.
- Apply the 3B's Principle™ - Brace, Breath and Body Position.
- Breathe in as you bend the elbows and lower both arms to the side of head keeping upper arm vertical and wrists straight at all times.
- Breathe out as you raise the dumbbells back up to the vertical starting position to complete one repetition.

Incline Single Arm Extension

| Start | Midpoint |

Instruction

- Lie on back on incline bench with feet resting on ground for support shoulder-width apart and right arm extended vertically with the left arm gripping rear of left triceps for support.
- Apply the 3B's Principle™ - Brace, Breath and Body Position.
- Breathe in as you bend the left elbow and lower dumbbell down to side of head keeping wrist straight at all times.
- Breathe out as you raise the dumbbell back up to the vertical starting position to complete one repetition.
- Repeat with opposite arm.

Standing Two Arm Extension

Start   Midpoint

Instruction
- Start in an upright standing position with feet shoulder-width apart and both arms extended vertically gripping either end of dumbbell – knuckles facing outwards.
- Apply 3B's Principle™ - Brace, Breath and Body Position.
- Breathe in as you bend the elbows and lower both arms until forearms descend just past parallel to the ground, behind your head.
- Breathe out as you raise the dumbbell back up to the vertical starting position to complete one repetition.
- Ensure strong abdominal brace at all times to avoid lower back arching.

Note: This exercise can also be performed seated on a flat weight bench or fitness ball or standing in a lunge position to reduce any stress on the lower back region when performing this exercise.

Standing Single Arm Extension

Start   Midpoint

Instruction

- Start in an upright standing position with feet shoulder-width apart and right arm extended vertically with the left arm gripping rear of left triceps for support – knuckles facing outwards.
- Apply 3B's Principle™ - Brace, Breath and Body Position.
- Breathe in as you bend the left elbow and lower until forearm descends just past parallel to the ground, beside your head.
- Breathe out as you raise the dumbbell back up to the vertical starting position to complete one repetition.
- Repeat with opposite arm.
- Ensure strong abdominal brace at all times to avoid lower back arching.

Note: This exercise can also be performed seated on a flat weight bench or fitness ball or standing in a lunge position to reduce any stress on the lower back region when performing this exercise.

Seated Single Arm Extension

Start Midpoint

Instruction

- Sit on edge of flat weight bench in an upright position with knees bent and feet shoulder-width apart and right arm extended vertically gripping dumbbell – knuckles facing outwards – and left hand resting behind rear of left triceps for support.
- Apply 3B's Principle™ - Brace, Breath and Body Position.
- Breathe in as you bend the elbow and lower arm until forearm descends just past parallel to the ground, behind your head.
- Breathe out as you raise the dumbbell back up to the vertical starting position to complete one repetition.
- Repeat with opposite arm.
- Ensure strong abdominal brace at all times to avoid lower back arching.

Note: This exercise can also be performed standing or seated on a fitness ball.

Standing Single Dumbbell Extension

Start   Midpoint

Instruction

- Start in an upright standing position with feet shoulder-width apart and both arms extended vertically gripping the underside of vertical dumbbell – palms facing upwards.
- Apply 3B's Principle™ - Brace, Breath and Body Position.
- Breathe in as you bend the elbows and lower until forearms descend just past parallel to the ground, behind your head.
- Breathe out as you raise the dumbbell back up to the vertical starting position to complete one repetition.
- Ensure strong abdominal brace at all times to avoid lower back arching.

Note: This exercise can also be performed seated on a flat weight bench or fitness ball or standing in a lunge position to reduce any stress on the lower back region when performing this exercise.

Fitness Ball Single Dumbbell Extension

Start   Midpoint

Instruction

- Sit on middle of fitness ball in an upright position with knees bent and feet shoulder width apart and both arms extended vertically gripping the underside of vertical dumbbell – palms facing upwards.
- Apply 3B's Principle™ - Brace, Breath and Body Position.
- Breathe in as you bend the elbows and lower until forearms descend just past parallel to the ground, behind your head.
- Breathe out as you raise the dumbbell back up to the vertical starting position to complete one repetition.
- Ensure strong abdominal brace at all times to avoid lower back arching.

Note: This exercise can also be performed kneeling, seated on a flat weight bench or standing in a lunge stance.

Lying Cross Face Extensions

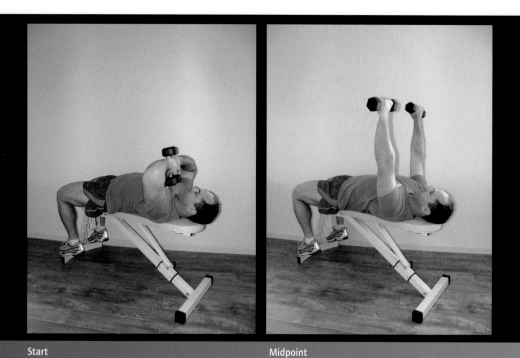

Start   Midpoint

Instruction

- Lie on back on flat weight bench with feet resting on ground for support shoulder width apart and both arms extended vertically and parallel gripping dumbbells – thumbs facing inwards.
- Apply the 3B's Principle™ - Brace, Breath and Body Position.
- Breathe in as you bend the elbows and lower both dumbbells inwards and down towards upper chest region with knuckles facing inwards and almost together.
- Breathe out as you raise the dumbbells back up to the vertical starting position to complete one repetition.

Note: This exercise can also be performed one arm at a time or using a single dumbbell with arm supported by the other.

BACK

The following exercises target both the back and arm muscles. Exercises include movement through the shoulder blades, shoulder girdle, elbow and wrist joints. The primary muscles used include:

- **Trapezius** – Upper portion of the back, sometimes referred to as 'traps' (upper trapezius) – the muscle running from the back of the neck to the shoulder.

- **Latissimus dorsi** – Large muscles of the mid-back. When properly trained they give the back a nice V shape, making the waist appear smaller. Exercise examples include pull-ups, chin-ups and pull-downs.

- **Deltoids** – The cap of the shoulder. This muscle has three parts, anterior deltoid (the front), medial deltoid (the middle), and posterior deltoid (the rear). Different movements target the different heads.

- **Rhomboids** – Muscles in the middle of the upper back between the shoulder blades. They're worked during chin-ups and other moves that bring the shoulder blades together.

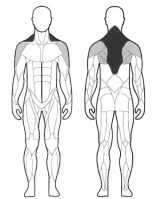

MUSCLES WORKED

■ **PRIMARY**
Upper Back

■ **SECONDARY**
Shoulders

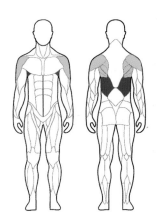

MUSCLES WORKED

■ **PRIMARY**
Mid-Back

■ **SECONDARY**
Shoulders

Double Arm Row – Neutral Grip

Start   Midpoint

Instruction

- Stand tall with feet hip-width apart gripping dumbbells at arm's length by your side.
- Bend at the hip and knee regions whilst leaning torso forwards until almost parallel to the ground with arms extended down – knuckles facing outwards.
- Apply 3B's Principle™ - Brace, Breath and Body Position.
- Keep your head, neck and back in neutral position at all times.
- Breathe out as you pull both arms up by bending at the elbows and raising high – keeping the arms close to the body.
- Breathe in as you lower the arms to complete one repetition.

Double Arm Row – Wide Grip

Start   Midpoint

Instruction

- Stand tall with feet hip-width apart gripping dumbbells at arm's length in front of thighs.
- Bend at the hip and knee regions whilst leaning torso forwards until almost parallel to the ground with arms extended down – knuckles facing forwards.
- Apply 3B's Principle™ - Brace, Breath and Body Position.
- Keep your head, neck and back in neutral position at all times.
- Breathe out as you pull both arms up by taking elbows up and out wide until upper arms are parallel to ground.
- Breathe in as you lower the arms to complete one repetition.

Bent Over Fly

Start   Midpoint

Instruction

- Stand tall with feet hip-width apart gripping dumbbells at arm's length by your side.
- Bend at the hip and knee regions whilst leaning torso forwards until almost parallel to the ground with arms extended down in front of body and slightly bent – knuckles facing outwards.
- Apply 3B's Principle™ - Brace, Breath and Body Position.
- Keep your head, neck and back in neutral position at all times.
- Breathe out as raise both arms up out wide in arching motion until upper arms are parallel to ground.
- Breathe in as you lower the arms to complete one repetition.

High Bench Rows

| Start | Midpoint |

Instruction

- Lie face down on high/incline bench with arms extended down gripping dumbbells – knuckles facing forwards.
- Apply 3B's Principle™ - Brace, Breath and Body Position.
- Breathe out as you bend your elbows and draw the dumbbells up towards the bench – keeping your elbows close to the body.
- Breathe in as you lower the dumbbells to full arms length to complete one repetition.

Exercise Variations Include:
Exercise Grip Variations:
- Knuckles facing outwards.
- Knuckles facing forwards.
- Knuckles facing backwards.

Bench options for the above 3 grip variations:
- Lying prone on High Flat Bench.
- Lying on stomach on Incline Bench.
- Lying on chest on Fitness Ball.

Single Arm Row

Start   Midpoint

Instruction

- Gripping dumbbell in left hand, kneel on flat weight bench with right knee and right hand.
- Position right shoulder directly over right hand whilst establishing a flat back and left arm gripping dumbbell extended down by side of bench – knuckles facing outwards.
- Apply 3B's Principle™ - Brace, Breath and Body Position.
- Breathe out as you bend your elbows and draw the dumbbells up towards the bench – keeping your elbows close to the body.
- Breathe out as you pull the dumbbell up toward your chest – keeping your elbow close to your body.
- Breathe in as you lower the dumbbell to arms length to complete one repetition.
- Repeat movement on opposite side.

Note: This exercise can also be performed without a bench by standing in a forward lunge position and resting hand on knee.

Lineman Row

Start   Midpoint

Instruction
- Stand tall with feet wider than shoulder-width apart gripping a single dumbbell at arm's length in front of body.
- Bend at the hip and knee regions whilst leaning torso forwards until almost parallel to the ground; with single arm at ankle level – knuckles facing outwards and opposite hand resting on knee.
- Apply 3B's Principle™ - Brace, Breath and Body Position.
- Keep your head, neck and back in neutral position at all times.
- Breathe out as you pull the single dumbbell up past the body, leading with the elbow – keeping the arms close to the body at all times.
- Breathe in as you lower the arm to complete one repetition.
- Repeat drill with dumbbell in opposite hand.

Note: Brace core and extend resting arm out wide for additional core challenge.

Pullovers

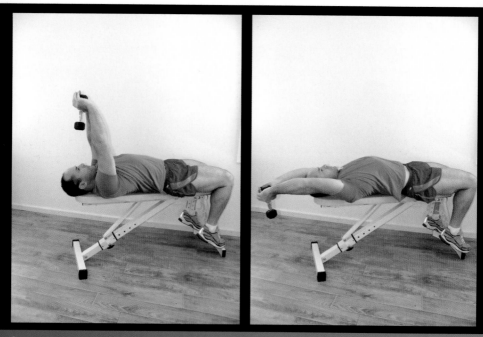

Start   Midpoint

Instruction

- Lie on back on flat weight bench with arms extended vertically with slight bend and both hands gripping the upper end of a single dumbbell – palms facing upwards – and knees bent with feet resting on the ground.
- Apply 3B's Principle™ - Brace, Breath and Body Position.
- Breathe in as you lower your arms overhead in an arch motion whilst resisting any arching of the lower back until the upper arms rest beside your ears.
- Breathe out as you pull the dumbbell back up overhead to complete one repetition.

Note: This exercise can also be performed lying across flat bench on upper back with knees bent and hips held high or on a fitness ball.

Fitness Ball Pullovers

Start   Midpoint

Instruction

- Lie on back on fitness ball with upper back region, arms extended vertically with slight bend and both hands gripping the upper end of a single dumbbell – palms facing upwards – and knees bent with feet resting on the ground.
- Apply 3B's Principle™ - Brace, Breath and Body Position – keeping hip position high in line with knees and shoulders.
- Breathe in as you lower your arms overhead in an arch motion whilst resisting any arching of the lower back until the upper arms rest beside your ears.
- Breathe out as you pull the dumbbell back up overhead to complete one repetition.

105

Upright Rows – Close Grip

Start   Midpoint

Instruction

- Start in an upright standing position with feet shoulder-width apart and arms extended down in front of thighs gripping dumbbells – close together – knuckles facing forwards.
- Apply 3B's Principle™ - Brace, Breath and Body Position.
- Leading with the elbows, breathe out as you raise the elbows up high whilst keeping the dumbbells close to the body up to chest height (under the chin).
- Avoid any forward raising of the dumbbells or bending of the wrists.
- Breathe in and lower to complete one repetition.

Note: This exercise can also be performed with a wider starting grip and raised position.

Standing Shrug

Start · Midpoint

Instruction

- Start in an upright standing position with feet shoulder-width apart and arms extended down to side of body with knuckles facing outwards.
- Apply 3B's Principle™ - Brace, Breath and Body Position.
- Leading with the shoulders, breathe out as you raise the shoulders up high whilst keeping the dumbbells close to the side of the body.
- Breathe in and lower to complete one repetition.

Note: This exercise can also be performed sitting on a flat bench or fitness ball.

Seated Shrug

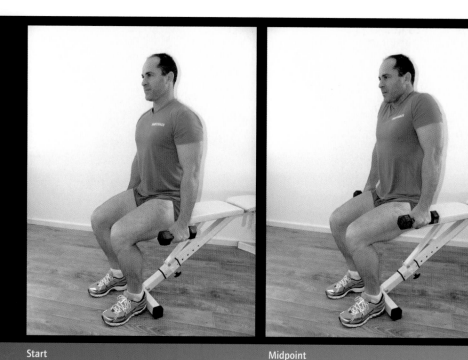

Start   Midpoint

Instruction

- Sit tall at the end of a flat weight bench with knees bent and feet resting on the ground and arms extended down to side of body with knuckles facing outwards.
- Apply 3B's Principle™ - Brace, Breath and Body Position.
- Leading with the shoulders, breathe out as you raise the shoulders up high whilst keeping the dumbbells close to the side of the body.
- Breathe in and lower to complete one repetition.

  Note: This exercise can also be performed sitting on a fitness ball or leaning forwards onto an inline bench for a mid back shrug.

Note: This exercise can also be performed standing, kneeling or seated on a fitness ball.

Incline Mid Back Shrug

Start   Midpoint

Instruction

- Lean forward and rest chest and torso on incline bench with feet resting on the ground and arms extended down to side of body with knuckles facing outwards.
- Apply 3B's Principle™ - Brace, Breath and Body Position.
- Leading with the shoulder blades, aim to squeeze them in together and lift up high as you breathe out.
- Pause briefly at the top.
- Breathe in and lower to complete one repetition.

Note: This exercise can also be performed lying prone (on stomach) on a high flat bench to vary muscle fiber activation.

CHEST

Strengthening the chest and arms in unison with the abdominal region plays a major role in body balance between the upper and lower body. The basic rule for all chest exercises is the narrower the hand position and movement, the greater the triceps contribution and the lesser the chest contribution; conversely, the wider the hand or movement angle position, the greater the chest contribution and the lesser the triceps contribution. The primary muscles targeted are:

- **Pectoralis (Chest)** – Large fan-shaped muscle that covers the front of the upper chest.

- **Triceps** – The rear side of the upper arm.

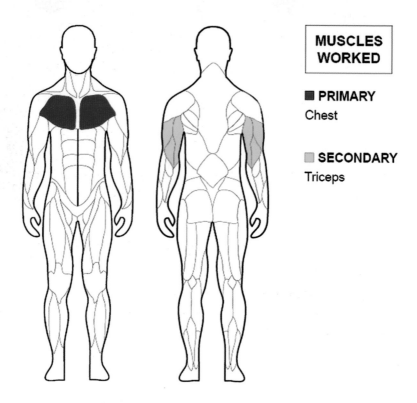

MUSCLES WORKED

■ **PRIMARY**
Chest

☐ **SECONDARY**
Triceps

Flat Bench Fly

Start   Midpoint

Instruction

- Lie on back on flat weight bench with feet resting on ground for support shoulder width apart and both arms extended vertically, though slightly bent, holding dumbbells – hands close with knuckles facing outwards.
- Apply the 3B's Principle™ - Brace, Breath and Body Position.
- Breathe in as you simultaneously lower both arms in a semi-circular motion, keeping arms in fixed position, until dumbbells are level with your chest.
- Breathe out as you raise the dumbbells back up to the starting position to complete one repetition.

Note: An additional hand rotation that twists the arms and palms back overhead in the upwards motion can also be used for additional chest activation.

Incline Bench Fly

Start   Midpoint

Instruction

- Lie on back on incline weight bench with feet resting on ground for support shoulder-width apart and both arms extended vertically, though slightly bent, holding dumbbells – hands close with knuckles facing outwards.
- Apply the 3B's Principle™ - Brace, Breath and Body Position.
- Breathe in as you simultaneously lower both arms in a semi-circular motion, keeping arms in fixed position, until dumbbells are level with your chest.
- Breathe out as you raise the dumbbells back up to the starting position to complete one repetition.

Note: This exercise can also be performed in an incline position on a fitness ball, by lowering hips towards ground with torso positioned at approximately 45 degrees. The fitness ball can be rested against wall for additional support.

Decline Bench Fly

| Start | Midpoint |

Instruction
- Lie on back on decline weight bench with feet supported (as per bench set-up) and both arms extended vertically, though slightly bent, holding dumbbells – hands close with knuckles facing outwards.
- Apply the 3B's Principle™ - Brace, Breath and Body Position.
- Breathe in as you simultaneously lower both arms in a semi-circular motion, keeping arms in fixed position, until dumbbells are level with your chest.
- Breathe out as you raise the dumbbells back up to the starting position to complete one repetition.

Flat Bench Fly Rotation

Start   Midpoint

Instruction

- Lie on back on flat weight bench with feet resting on ground for support shoulder-width apart and both arms extended vertically, though slightly bent, holding dumbbells with palms facing back overhead and ends of dumbbells together.
- Apply the 3B's Principle™ - Brace, Breath and Body Position.
- Breathe in as you simultaneously lower both arms in a semi-circular motion whilst rotating the knuckles outwards, keeping arms in fixed position, until dumbbells are level with your chest.
- Breathe out as you raise the dumbbells back up to the starting position to complete one repetition.

Note: This exercise can also be performed on an incline bench, decline bench and fitness ball.

Fitness Ball Flyes

Start   Midpoint

Instruction

- Lie on back and shoulders on Fitness Ball with feet resting on ground for support shoulder width apart and both arms extended vertically, though slightly bent, holding dumbbells – hands close with knuckles facing outwards.
- With hips raised and body aligned from shoulders to knees, apply the 3B's Principle™ - Brace, Breath and Body Position.
- Breathe in as you simultaneously lower both arms in a semi-circular motion, keeping arms in fixed position, until dumbbells are level with your chest.
- Breathe out as you raise the dumbbells back up to the starting position to complete one repetition.

Note: This exercise can also be performed in an incline position on a fitness ball, by lowering hips towards ground with torso positioned at approximately 45 degrees. The fitness ball can be rested against wall for additional support.

Flat Bench Press

| Start | Midpoint |

Instruction

- Lie on back on flat weight bench with feet resting on ground for support shoulder-width apart and both arms extended vertically, holding dumbbells − palms upwards, ends of dumbbells close together.
- Apply the 3B's Principle™ - Brace, Breath and Body Position.
- Breathe in as you simultaneously lower both arms by bending the elbows until dumbbells are level with your chest.
- Breathe out as you raise the dumbbells back up to the starting position to complete one repetition.

Note: A Hammer Grip, palms facing each other with hands resting above shoulders, can also be used, though more emphasis is now placed on the triceps muscles by keeping elbows close to the body when lowering and raising arms.

Incline Bench Press

Start   Midpoint

Instruction

- Lie on back on incline weight bench with feet resting on ground for support shoulder-width apart and both arms extended vertically, holding dumbbells – hands close with knuckles facing outwards.
- Apply the 3B's Principle™ - Brace, Breath and Body Position.
- Breathe in as you simultaneously lower both arms by bending the elbows until dumbbells are level with your chest.
- Breathe out as you raise the dumbbells back up to the starting position to complete one repetition.

Variation: This exercise can also be performed in an incline position on a fitness ball, by lowering hips towards ground with torso positioned at approximately 45 degrees. The fitness ball can be rested against wall for additional support.

Note: A Hammer Grip, palms facing each other with hands resting above shoulders, can also be used, though more emphasis is now placed on the triceps muscles by keeping elbows close to the body when lowering and raising arms.

Decline Bench Press

Start   Midpoint

Instruction
- Lie on back on decline weight bench with feet supported (as per bench set-up) and both arms extended vertically holding dumbbells – palms upwards, ends of dumbbells close together.
- Apply the 3B's Principle™ - Brace, Breath and Body Position.
- Breathe in as you simultaneously lower both arms by bending the elbows until dumbbells are level with your chest.
- Breathe out as you raise the dumbbells back up to the starting position to complete one repetition.

Note: A Hammer Grip, palms facing each other with hands resting above shoulders, can also be used, though more emphasis is now placed on the triceps muscles by keeping elbows close to the body when lowering and raising arms.

Fitness Ball Bench Press

Start   Midpoint

Instruction
- Lie on back and shoulders on Fitness Ball with feet resting on ground for support shoulder-width apart and both arms extended vertically, holding dumbbells – palms upwards, ends of dumbbells close together.
- Apply the 3B's Principle™ - Brace, Breath and Body Position
- Breathe in as you simultaneously lower both arms by bending the elbows until dumbbells are level with your chest.
- Breathe out as you raise the dumbbells back up to the starting position to complete one repetition

Note: A Hammer Grip, palms facing each other with hands resting above shoulders, can also be used, though more emphasis is now placed on the triceps muscles by keeping elbows close to the body when lowering and raising arms

Variation: This exercise can also be performed in an incline position on a Fitness Ball, by lowering hips towards ground with torso positioned at approximately 45 degrees. The fitness Ball can be rested against wall for additional support.

Alternate Flat Bench Press 2+1

Start

Midpoint

In motion

Instruction

- Lie on back on flat weight bench with feet resting on ground for support shoulder-width apart and both arms extended vertically, holding dumbbells – palms upwards, ends of dumbbells close together.

- Apply the 3B's Principle™ - Brace, Breath and Body Position.

- Breathe in as you lower one dumbbell by bending the elbow until the dumbbell is level with your chest – ensuring your core is held strong.

- Breathe out as you alternate the arm movement, simultaneously raising the lowered dumbbell back up and the other raised dumbbell down to your chest to complete one repetition.

Note: This exercise can also be performed on an Incline Bench or Fitness Ball. Additional variations include lowering and raising one arm, before repeating with the other. A Hammer Grip, palms facing each other with hands resting above shoulders, can also be used, though more emphasis is now placed on the triceps muscles.

See Stage 2: Functional Exercises for additional chest variations

LEGS

Teaching Points

- Apply 3B's Principle™ - Brace, Breath and Body Position with each exercise.
- Keep tall through the chest and aim to make movement flow efficiently.
- Keep knees over midline of toes.
- Ensure good ankle, knee, hip and body alignment is maintained when lowering and raising the body.
- Maintain a strong pelvic position parallel to ground at all times without allowing the pelvis tilt or lower on one side.
- Maintain deep breathing pattern at all times.
- Breathe out when rising.
- Breathe in when lowering.
- Stop exercise if any lower back or knee tension or pain arises.
- Always have coach or personal trainer assist in demonstrating, teaching and spotting each exercise.

This section combines the muscles of the leg and hip regions:

- **Quadriceps** – This is the large group of muscles on the front of the upper leg, often referred to as the thighs – starting at the hip joint and ending at the knee joint. Their primary function is to flex the hip and extend the knee, very important in walking, running, jumping, climbing and pedaling a bike.
- **Hamstrings** – This is the group of muscles on the back side of the leg, running from the hip joint to the knee joint. Their primary function is to facilitate flexion of legs, medial and lateral rotation, important for walking, running and jumping.
- **Gluteal Region** – Often referred to as the buttock region, the primary function is hip extension in unison with the hip stabilizers important in all lower body movements.
- **Lower Back** – There are several muscles in the lower back (lumbar region) that assist with rotation, flexibility and strength. It generally refers to the segment of the torso, between the diaphragm and the sacrum on the rear side of the body from which muscle and fascia attach.

Note: Additional dumbbell calf exercises are included on page 152-157.

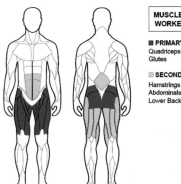

MUSCLES
WORKED

■ PRIMARY
Quadriceps
Glutes

□ SECONDARY
Hamstrings
Abdominals
Lower Back

Deadlifts

Deadlifts

Start   Midpoint

Instruction

- Start in a squat position with feet shoulder-width apart, back flat and arms extended down in front of body outside of knees with knuckles facing forwards.
- The key starting point for the dumbbells in this exercise is mid shin level when in a squat position – imitating the starting position of an Olympic Lift if using a barbell.
- Apply 3B's Principle™ - Brace, Breath and Body Position.
- Driving through the legs, push the body up until your legs are straight.
- Ensure the dumbbells remain close to your legs as you rise.
- Once standing, pause briefly, then reverse the movement back down to the starting position to complete one repetition.

Wheelbarrow Deadlift

Start   Midpoint

Instruction

- Start in a squat position with feet shoulder-width apart, back flat and arms extended down outside legs around ankle height with knuckles facing outwards – as if you were holding wheelbarrow handles though in a lower starting position.
- The range of motion through the hip and lower back region in a squat position will depend on one's flexibility, coordination and muscle control.
- Apply 3B's Principle™ - Brace, Breath and Body Position.
- Driving through the legs, push the body up until your legs are straight.
- Ensure the dumbbells remain close to your legs as you rise.
- Once standing, pause briefly, then reverse the movement back down to the starting position to complete one repetition.

Straight-leg Deadlift

Start   Midpoint

Instruction
- Start in an upright standing position, arms extended down and dumbbells resting on thighs with knuckles facing forwards.
- Applying the 3B's Principle™, brace the core-abdominal muscles.
- Keeping your back flat and legs straight, bend forward at the hips, lowering the body until the torso is parallel to the ground.
- Ensure your head and neck remain neutral to your body and avoid lowering the dumbbells below mid shin level – imitating the end point if using an Olympic bar with plates.
- Once lowered, pause briefly, then reverse the movement back up ensuring the abdominals remain braced back up to the starting position to complete one repetition.

Sumo Deadlift

Start | Midpoint

Instruction

- Using a single dumbbell, rest it up on one end.
- Standing over dumbbell, lower down in a sumo squat position with feet wider than shoulder-width apart, gripping upper side of dumbbell with both hands – knuckles towards the ground.
- Apply 3B's Principle™ - Brace, Breath and Body Position.
- Driving through the legs, push the body up until standing tall with the arms remaining straight at all times and close to the body.
- Once standing, pause briefly, then reverse the movement back down to the starting position to complete one repetition.

Single-Leg Deadlift

Start   Midpoint

Instruction

- Gripping dumbbells in each hand by your side – knuckles facing outwards – balance on the left leg with the right leg raised slightly off ground behind the body.
- Apply 3B's Principle™ - Brace, Breath and Body Position.
- Keeping your back flat and legs straight bend forward at the hips, lowering the body until the torso is parallel to the ground.
- To increase the challenge also raise the rear leg until parallel ensuring the hips remain square.
- Ensure your head and neck remain neutral to your body whilst the arms are extended down.
- Once lowered, pause briefly, then reverse the movement back up ensuring the hips remain square and abdominals braced back up to the starting position to complete one repetition.
- Ensure good ankle, knee, hip and body alignment is maintained when lowering and raising the torso and rear leg.
- Repeat movement balancing on right leg.

Good Morning

Start   Midpoint

Instruction

- Stand tall with feet shoulder-width apart, locking dumbbells against body at shoulder height – knuckles facing outwards.
- Apply 3B's Principle™ - Brace, Breath and Body Position.
- Lower upper body forwards by pushing your hips back and slightly bending knees until your back is parallel to the ground.
- Once lowered, pause briefly, then reverse the movement back up to the starting position to complete one repetition.
- Ensure head and neck remain neutral with the body at all times.

This exercise strengthens the hamstrings, glutes and lower back regions.

Lunges

Arm and hand positioning plays a major role in determining the challenge placed on the legs and core region in lunge exercises.

Six variations of arm positioning include:

1. Arms extended down by side gripping dumbbells – knuckles facing outwards.

2. Arms extended forwards of the body gripping dumbbells – arms parallel to ground; knuckles facing upwards.

3. Arms extended out laterally to the side of the body gripping dumbbells – arms parallel to ground; thumbs facing upwards.

4. Dumbbells resting on front of shoulders – palms and elbows parallel – knuckles facing outwards.

5. Arms bent at shoulder level with forearms facing forwards and dumbbells positioned slightly above shoulder level – knuckles facing backwards.

6. Arms fully extended overhead gripping dumbbells – close or wide grip – with knuckles facing backwards or outwards.

This arm positioning also adds an isometric strength element to the arm, upper back and shoulder regions. In addition, some exercises allow movement pattern to be included from a shoulder position to overhead position, for example, whilst performing an alternate leg lunge or a single arm option. In general, these exercise variations are included in Stage 2 – Functional Exercises.

As with any exercise, stop the exercise immediately or re-adjust the body constantly using the 3B's Principle™ once the core brace is lost or fatigue sets in. Always apply quality of movement over quantity.

Stationary Lunge

Start | Midpoint

Instruction

- Stand tall in forward lunge position – one leg forward and the other back behind body resting on toes – arms extended down resting dumbbells by your side.
- Tilt pelvis back, brace abdominals and square hips for to ensure correct torso positioning during movement and avoiding any arching of the lower back region.
- Apply the 3B's Principle™ - Brace, Breath and Body Position.
- Breathe in as you lower rear knee towards the ground and front thigh reaches parallel to the ground – knees over toes.
- Breathe out and rise up to complete one repetition.
- Repeat drill with opposite leg forward.

Note: For additional challenge see arm positioning options on page 128.

Overhead Stationary Lunge

Start   Midpoint

Instruction

- Stand tall in forward lunge position with arms extended overhead holding dumbbells – knuckles facing backwards (or inwards).
- Tilt pelvis back, brace abdominals and square hips to ensure correct torso positioning during movement and avoiding any arching of the lower back region.
- Apply the 3B's Principle™ - Brace, Breath and Body Position.
- Breathe in and lower rear knee towards ground – keeping pelvis square and knees over toes until front thigh is parallel.
- Breathe out and rise up again to complete one repetition.
- Repeat set with opposite leg forward.

Note: A single dumbbell can also be used as a variation to this exercise – opposite arm to forward leg.

Alternate Leg Lunge

Start   Midpoint

Instruction

- Stand tall with feet close together and arms extended down resting dumbbells by your side.
- Apply the 3B's Principle™ - Brace, Breath and Body Position.
- Breathe in as you step forwards with one leg into a lunge position until front thigh is parallel to the ground and knee over toes.
- Breathe out and rise back up to starting position to complete one repetition.
- Repeat drill with opposite leg lunging forward.

Variation: This exercise can also be performed in a forward walking lunge movement pattern. For additional challenge see arm positioning options on page 128.

Diagonal Lunge

Start   Midpoint

Instruction

- Stand tall with feet close together and arms extended down resting dumbbells by your side.
- Apply the 3B's Principle™ - Brace, Breath and Body Position.
- Breathe in as you step across diagonally at a 45-degree angle with one leg into a lunge position until front thigh is parallel to the ground and knee positioned over toes.
- Breathe out and rise back up to starting position, pushing off forward leg, to complete one repetition.
- Repeat drill with opposite leg lunging diagonally.

Note: This drill can also be performed with the whole body, including rear foot and chest and shoulders, turning at a 45-degree angle to starting point. For additional challenge see arm positioning options on page 128.

Side Lunge

Start   Midpoint

Instruction

- Stand tall with feet close together and arms extended down resting dumbbells by your side.
- Apply the 3B's Principle™ - Brace, Breath and Body Position.
- Breathe in as you step out to side of body (laterally) with one leg into a lunge position, foot facing forwards until front thigh is parallel to the ground and knee positioned over toes and rear leg straight.
- Ensure torso remains forwards and upright and hips square.
- Breathe out and rise back up to starting position, pushing off forward leg, to complete one repetition.
- Repeat drill, lunging to opposite side.

Note: For additional challenge see arm positioning options on page 128.

Backward Lunge

Start   Step Back

Instruction

- Stand tall with feet close together and arms extended down resting dumbbells by your side.
- Apply the 3B's Principle™ - Brace, Breath and Body Position.
- Breathe in as you step backwards with one leg into a lunge position until front thigh is parallel to the ground and knee over toes.
- Breathe out and rise back up to starting position to complete one repetition.
- Repeat drill with opposite leg lunging backwards.

Note: For additional challenge see arm positioning options on page 128.

Raised Lunge

Start   Midpoint

Instruction

- Stand tall in a lunge position with rear foot raised onto bench and arms extended down resting dumbbells by your side.
- Tilt pelvis back, brace abdominals and square hips for to ensure correct torso positioning during movement.
- Apply the 3B's Principle™ - Brace, Breath and Body Position.
- Breathe in as lower rear knee towards the ground and front thigh reaches parallel to the ground – knee over toes.
- Breathe out and rise up to complete one repetition.
- Repeat drill with opposite leg forward.

Note: For additional challenge see arm positioning options on page 128.

Raised Stability Lunge

Start | Midpoint

Instruction

- Stand tall in a lunge position with rear foot raised onto Fitness Ball and arms extended down resting dumbbells by your side.
- Tilt pelvis back, brace abdominals and square hips for to ensure correct torso positioning during movement.
- Apply the 3B's Principle™ - Brace, Breath and Body Position – for core control with rear foot on Fitness Ball.
- Breathe in as lower rear knee towards the ground and front thigh reaches parallel to the ground – knee over toes.
- Breathe out and rise up to complete one repetition.
- Ensure hips remain square at all times.
- Repeat drill with opposite leg forward.

Note: For additional challenge see arm positioning options on page 128.

Step Ups

| Start | Midpoint | Raised |

Instruction
- Stand tall with feet close together one step back from flat weight bench.
- Arms are extended down resting dumbbells by your side.
- Apply the 3B's Principle™ - Brace, Breath and Body Position.
- Step one foot up onto bench, then follow up with the other – standing tall on top of bench.
- Pause, before reversing motion stepping one foot back then the other.
- Repeat drill with opposite leg stepping up first.

Note: For additional challenge see arm positioning options on page 128.

Single-Leg Drives

Start   Midpoint

Instruction

- Stand in forward lunge position with one foot resting up on flat weight bench and arms extended down resting dumbbells by your side.
- Apply the 3B's Principle™ - Brace, Breath and Body Position.
- Keeping pelvis square, breathe out as your drive up to straighten forward leg.
- Ensure forward leg maintains the majority of weight-bearing throughout movement.
- Breath-in and lower in a controlled motion – keeping upper body leaning slightly forward to maintain tension on forward leg to complete one repetition.
- Repeat drill on opposite leg.

Note: For additional challenge see arm positioning options on page 128.

Lateral Step Overs

Instruction

- Stand side on to flat weight bench with arms bent and dumbbells resting at shoulder height.
- Apply the 3B's Principle™ - Brace, Breath and Body Position.
- Step inside leg up sideways onto bench followed by the other before stepping down across to the opposite side.
- Repeat drill from other side up and over again – up, up, down, down movement pattern.
- The speed of movement is determined by the weight used. For example: heavy dumbbells for a slower, more controlled movement pattern to build strength as opposed to a light pair of dumbbells that are used for a more rapid transition.

Note: For additional challenge see arm positioning options on page 128.

Additional functional lunge combinations are found in Stage 2.

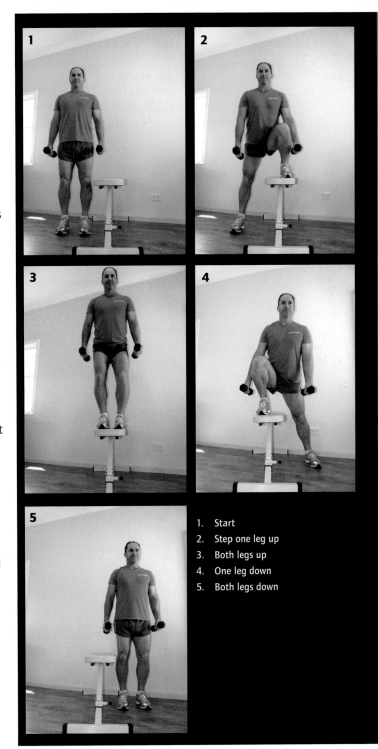

1. Start
2. Step one leg up
3. Both legs up
4. One leg down
5. Both legs down

Squats

Squat Patterning

The squat exercise is the foundation movement for a wide variety of sporting skills from exploding out of the blocks in the 100m dash to jumping, landing and stepping. The squat itself is a highly effective measure of muscular balance, coordination and flexibility due to the requirement of depth, control and body positioning.

The squat movement generally ranges from a half squat (90-degree leg angle) to a full or deep squat position required in Olympic Lifting. Working between these ranges will depend on one's coordination, strength, control and flexibility. These elements along with a person's age and biomechanical efficiency need to be taken into consideration with the actual squat depth performed and will need to be assessed and approved by a physical therapist or qualified strength and conditioning coach or personal trainer. This is designed to protect one's lower back, knee and ankle regions from injury.

Once a good squat pattern is obtained through body weight movements and stretching (or stability drills), the weight of dumbbells used can be increased for strength improvements. Always apply the 3B's Principle™ to ensure correct body posture, breathing and movement patterns in the squat exercises.

Good Body Alignment

Ultimately one's goal in squatting is to effectively activate the glutes, hamstrings and thigh muscles. This is achieved through initial activation of the hip and knee region by pushing the glutes back and keeping the back flat whilst the knees remain over the toes from a side and front perspective.

Good Squat Alignment
Side Position
- Ear over shoulder
- Shoulder over knee
- Knee over toes
- Flat feet on ground

Front position
- Knees aligned with toes
- Weight across footprint

Good Postural Alignment

The most common faults to avoid in squatting are:

- **Bending primarily at the ankles first** – as this limits range of motion at this joint and leads to the heels rising off the ground or knees rolling inwards to accommodate any further squatting movement to occur. This may also lead to a more upright body position as opposed to shoulder over knee. For this reason, participants with flat feet, weak knees or poor squat initiation at the ankles need to concentrate on keeping their weight across their foot print (establishing a foot arch) and centered; knees aligned over the toes with initial activation at the hip and knees region simultaneously (as shown in photo above).
- **Bending too far forward at the hips** – as this leads to overloading the lower back region.

The squat itself is a key functional movement pattern. So to improve these faults described above and others, you can practice the supported squat exercise to learn good technique, as follows.

Supported Squat

| Start | Midpoint |

Instruction

- To assist with squat development, stand next to a pole (or frame).
- Stand with feet shoulder-width apart, holding pole with both hands.
- Apply the 3B's Principle™ and establish good foot arch and knee alignment by bringing awareness to the movement that follows.
- Using hands as a support guide only, simultaneously bend at the hips and knees and lower body pushing the gluteus back whilst shoulders remain over knees, and knees over toes – trailing the hands down pole with your body for initial support.
- Keep head close to pole when lowering and focus on adjusting body to maintain a good body position – ear over shoulder, over knee, over toes.

Note:

- Using a pole for support enables you to improve the technical aspect of squatting by forcing you to push back through your glutes whilst limiting bending too far forwards at the hip and shoulders – instead establishing good body alignment.
- This is a great warm-up drill prior to any exercise, especially free weight training. Once competent, move away from pole and repeat the squat movement using one's body weight only with arms extended forwards parallel to ground.
- Master this drill before adding any weight to the squat movement.
- Ensure regular stretching and massage for maintaining good muscle pliability for all exercises.
- Lower down initially into short range of motion until strength and flexibility or stability improves. Gradually lower deeper as muscles and joints allow, under the guidance of a physical therapist or qualified coach.

Bench Squat

| Start | Midpoint |

Instruction

- Start in an upright standing position in front of a weight bench, with arms extended down by side gripping dumbbells and feet shoulder-width apart.
- Apply 3B's Principle™ - Brace, Breath and Body Position whilst aligning feet and knees for natural foot arch and good alignment.
- Breathing in, slowly squat down by simultaneously bending at the hip, knees and ankles whilst maintaining a flat back position.
- Lower body down until your glutes touch the bench – thighs almost parallel to the ground – arms remain straight.
- The bench is just a reminder of your end point when lowering, so as soon as you touch it rise straight up again – avoid any sitting or unloading.
- Breathe out as you raise your body upwards using your legs to starting position to complete one repetition.
- Ensure your heels remain on the floor and knees aligned over the toes at all times.

Note: For additional challenge see arm positioning options on page 128.

Single Leg Bench Squat

Start   Midpoint

Instruction

- Start in an upright standing position in front of a weight bench, with arms extended down by side gripping dumbbells and one foot raised slightly off the ground in front of the body.

- Apply 3B's Principle™ - Brace, Breath and Body Position whilst aligning feet and knees for natural foot arch and good alignment.

- Breathing in, slowly squat down by simultaneously bending at the hip, knees and ankles whilst maintaining a flat back and ensuring hips remain square and knee aligned over the toes.

- Lower body down until your glutes touch the bench – thighs almost parallel to the ground – arms remain straight.

- The bench is just a reminder of your end point when lowering, so soon as you touch it rise straight up again – avoid any sitting or unloading.

- Breathe out as you raise your body upwards using your legs to starting position to complete one repetition.

- Repeat single leg bench squat on opposite leg.

Note: For additional challenge see arm positioning options on page 128.

Squat

Start   Midpoint

Instruction

- Start in an upright standing position with feet shoulder-width apart and arms extended down by side gripping dumbbells.

- Apply 3B's Principle™ - Brace, Breath and Body Position whilst aligning feet and knees for natural foot arch and good alignment.

- Breathing in, slowly squat down to a half or full-squat position by simultaneously bending at the hip, knees and ankles whilst maintaining a flat back position and arms by your side at all times.

- Breathe out as you raise your body upwards, using your legs, to the starting position to complete one repetition.

- Keep your heels on the floor and knees following the line of your toes. Resist any additional leaning forward from the hips focusing on maintaining good body alignment – ear over shoulder, over hip, over ankle – from side position.

- See notes on page 140 in relation to appropriate depth of squat and good body alignment.

Note: For additional challenge see arm positioning options on page 128.

Sumo Squat

Start   Midpoint

Instruction

- Stand tall with feet wider than shoulder-width, arms extended downwards gripping the end of a single dumbbell in both hands vertically.
- Apply 3B's Principle™ - Brace, Breath and Body Position whilst aligning feet and knees for natural foot arch and good alignment.
- Breathe in whilst simultaneously bending the hip, knee and ankles and lowering the body until dumbbell comes near or touches the ground – keeping arms straight at all times.
- Breathe out and rise upwards to complete one repetition.

Front Squat – Single

Start   Midpoint

Instruction

- Start in an upright standing position with feet shoulder-width apart and hands gripping either end of a single dumbbell across your chest.
- Apply 3B's Principle™ - Brace, Breath and Body Position whilst aligning feet and knees for natural foot arch and good alignment.
- Breathing in, slowly squat down to a half or full-squat position by simultaneously bending at the hip, knees and ankles whilst maintaining a flat back position.
- Breathe out as you raise your body upwards, using your legs, to the starting position to complete one repetition.
- Look forward or above the horizon for better movement control with weight in front of body.
- See notes on page 140 in relation to appropriate depth of squat and good body alignment.

Front Squat – Double

Start   Midpoint

Instruction

- Start in an upright standing position with feet shoulder-width apart and hands gripping dumbbells in a bent arm position against your body at shoulder height.

- Apply 3B's Principle™ - Brace, Breath and Body Position whilst aligning feet and knees for natural foot arch and good alignment.

- Breathing in, slowly squat down to a half or full-squat position by simultaneously bending at the hip, knees and ankles whilst maintaining a flat back position and keeping dumbbells parallel and elbows high.

- Breathe out as you raise your body upwards, using your legs, to the starting position to complete one repetition.

- Look forward or above the horizon for better movement control with weight in front of body.

- See notes on page 140 in relation to appropriate depth of squat and good body alignment.

Overhead Squat

Instruction

- Start in an upright standing position with feet shoulder-width apart and hands gripping dumbbells overhead in extended position shoulder-width apart.

- Apply 3B's Principle™ - Brace, Breath and Body Position whilst aligning feet and knees for natural foot arch and good alignment.

- Breathing in, slowly squat down to a half or full-squat position by simultaneously bending at the hip, knees and ankles whilst maintaining a flat back position and keeping dumbbells extended overhead.

- Breathe out as you raise your body upwards, using your legs, to the starting position to complete one repetition.

- Look forward or above the horizon for better movement control with weight in front of body.

- Good shoulder flexibility and strength is required for muscle control of dumbbells. Hence, always start with light dumbbells and master exercise before progressing.

- See notes on page 140 in relation to appropriate depth of squat and good body alignment. Ensure good flexibility is achieved through the upper back and shoulder region for correct movement. See page 206 for Stretching Routine.

Start

Midpoint

Raised

Fitness Ball Squat

Start   Midpoint

Instruction

- Stand tall with feet shoulder-width apart and Fitness Ball against wall and rear of lower back region.
- Grip dumbbells in both hands – extended down by side of body at all times
- Apply 3B's Principle™ - Brace, Breath and Body Position whilst aligning feet and knees for natural foot arch and good alignment.
- Breathing in, slowly squat down to a half or full-squat position by pushing your glutes back under the ball as it rises up your back.
- Breathe out as you raise your body upwards, using your legs, to the starting position to complete one repetition.
- See notes on page 140 in relation to depth of squat and good body alignment.
- Focus on performing a normal squat movement pattern – adjust body and foot and knee position accordingly.

Note: For additional challenge see arm positioning options on page 128.

Single Leg Fitness Ball Squat

Start   Midpoint

Instruction

- Stand tall with feet shoulder-width apart and Fitness Ball against wall and rear of lower back region.
- Grip dumbbells in both hands – extended down by side of body at all times.
- Apply 3B's Principle™ - Brace, Breath and Body Position whilst aligning foot and knee for natural foot arch and good alignment.
- Raise on leg forward of the body off the ground whilst ensuring hips remain square at all times.
- Breathing in, slowly squat down to a half-squat position by pushing your glutes back under the ball as it rises up your back.
- Breathe out as you raise your body upwards, using your leg, to the starting position to complete one repetition.
- Repeat on opposite leg.
- See notes on page 140 in relation to depth of squat and good body alignment.
- Use light weights initially and shorter squat depth until you master this movement before adding weight or squatting lower.

Note: For additional challenge see arm positioning options on page 128.

CALVES

- **Calves** – The group of muscles on the back of the leg running from the backside of the knee to the Achilles tendon which bends the knee and points the toes (plantar flexion), helping us in walking, running, pedaling a bike and jumping.
- **Soleus** – The flat muscle underneath calf muscle which acts only on the ankle joint to also point the toes.

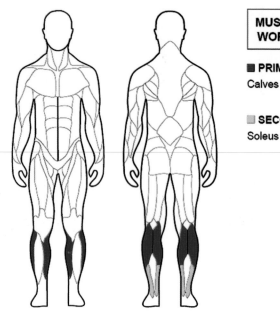

MUSCLES
WORKED

■ PRIMARY
Calves

■ SECONDARY
Soleus

Standing Calf Raise

Start   Midpoint

Instruction

- Stand tall with feet hip-width apart and arms extended down by side of body gripping dumbbells.
- Apply 3B's Principle™ - Brace, Breath and Body Position.
- Breathing out, simultaneously rise up onto the balls of both feet, raising your heels as high as possible without losing balance.
- Pause briefly at the top of movement before breathing in as you slowly lower your heels back down to the ground to complete one repetition.

Note: This exercise can also be performed with balls of both feet resting over the edge of step and raising and lowering. It can also be performed using one leg off the edge of a step.

Balance Calf-Raise

Start   Midpoint

Instruction

- Stand tall with feet hip-width apart and arms extended down by side of body gripping dumbbells.
- Raise one knee until parallel off the ground and apply the 3B's Principle™ - Brace, Breath and Body Position.
- Breathing out, rise up onto the ball of the foot, raising your heel as high as possible without losing balance.
- Pause briefly at the top of movement before breathing in as you slowly lower your heel back down to the ground to complete one repetition.
- Repeat with opposite leg.

Note: A single dumbbell may be used to allow support of the opposite hand until mastering the exercise or adding weight. Variations of hand positions can also challenge your core whilst strengthening the calf muscles.

Fitness Ball Wall Calf Raises

Start   Midpoint

Instruction

- In a standing position gripping dumbbells in both hands down by your side, lean your chest into the Fitness Ball against the wall.
- Apply 3B's Principle™ - Brace, Breath and Body Position.
- Breathing out, simultaneously rise up onto the balls of both feet, raising your heels as high as possible without losing balance.
- Pause briefly at the top of movement before breathing in as you slowly lower your heels back down to the ground to complete one repetition.

Seated Calf Raise

Start   Midpoint

Instruction

- Sit tall in middle of flat weight bench, with ball of feet positioned on edge of bench rails so that your heels are lowered towards ground and knees directly over ankles.

- Gripping dumbbells rest them on top of thigh near your knees in an upright (vertical) position with knuckles facing outwards.

- Maintaining a solid body position, simultaneously rise heels up by pushing up onto the balls of your feet.

- Pause briefly, then lower heels back down to the ground in a controlled manner to complete one repetition.

Seated Fitness Ball Calf Raise

Start

Midpoint

Instruction

- Sit tall in middle of Fitness Ball with feet hip-width apart.
- Gripping dumbbells, rest them on top of thigh near your knees in an upright (vertical) position with knuckles facing outwards.
- Maintaining a solid body position, simultaneously rise up onto the balls of your feet, before lowering heels back down to the ground to complete one repetition.

157

SHOULDERS

The deltoid (shoulder) muscle covers the shoulder and consists of three distinct segments:

1. The **anterior** or front deltoid allows you to raise your arm to the front.
2. The **medial** or middle deltoid allows you to raise your arm to the side.
3. The **posterior** or rear deltoid allows you to draw your arm backwards when it is perpendicular to the torso.

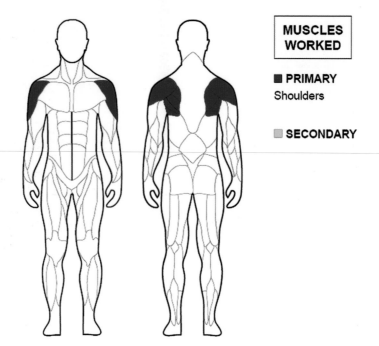

MUSCLES WORKED

■ PRIMARY
Shoulders

□ SECONDARY

Different exercise movements of the shoulder region target the different heads of the deltoid.

Reverse Fly

Start   Midpoint

Instruction

- Stand tall with feet hip-width apart gripping dumbbells at arm's length in front of thighs.
- Bend at the hip and knee regions whilst leaning torso forwards until almost parallel to the ground with arms extended down – knuckles facing outwards and arms slightly bent.
- Apply 3B's Principle™ - Brace, Breath and Body Position.
- Keep your head, neck and back in neutral position at all times.
- Breathe out as you raise the arms out wide in a semi-circular motion until upper arms are parallel to ground; maintaining slightly bent arms at all times.
- Breathe in as you lower the arms to complete one repetition strengthening the rear deltoid muscles.

High Bench Reverse Fly

Start | Midpoint

Instruction

- Lie face down on high bench with arms extended down gripping dumbbells – knuckles facing outwards and arms slightly bent.
- Apply 3B's Principle™ - Brace, Breath and Body Position.
- Keep your head, neck and back in neutral position at all times.
- Breathe out as you raise the arms out wide in a semi-circular motion until upper arms are parallel to ground; maintaining slightly bent arms at all times.
- Breathe in as you lower the arms to complete one repetition strengthening the rear deltoid muscles.

Note: This exercise can also be performed lying on a Fitness Ball.

Front Raise – Both Arms

Start   Midpoint

Instruction

- Start in an upright standing position with feet shoulder-width apart and arms extended down in front of thighs gripping dumbbells – close together – knuckles facing forwards.
- Apply 3B's Principle™ - Brace, Breath and Body Position.
- Breathe out as you raise the arms up in a semi-circular motion until arms are parallel to the ground – keeping wrists straight at all times.
- Breathe in and lower to complete one repetition.

Note: This exercise can also be performed in a seated position on an incline bench or in a reverse position with chest leaning against incline bench; as well as seated on a Fitness Ball or kneeling on the ground.

161

Front Raise – Alternate Arms

Start   Midpoint

Instruction

• Start in an upright standing position with feet shoulder-width apart and arms extended down in front of thighs gripping dumbbells – close together – knuckles facing forwards.

• Apply 3B's Principle™ - Brace, Breath and Body Position.

• Breathe out as you raise one arm up in a semi-circular motion until parallel to the ground – keeping wrists straight at all times.

• Breathe in and lower to complete one repetition, before raising the opposite arm.

Note: This exercise can also be performed in a seated position on an incline bench or in a reverse position with chest leaning against incline bench; as well as seated on a Fitness Ball or kneeling on the ground.

Standing Shoulder Press

Start   Midpoint

Instruction

- Stand tall with feet shoulder-width apart and arms bent and raised at the side of body at shoulder height with palms facing forwards.
- Apply 3B's Principle™ - Brace, Breath and Body Position
- Breathe out as you raise both dumbbells up overhead and in together with ends coming close together.
- Breathe in and lower back to shoulder height to complete one repetition.

Note: This exercise can also be performed sitting on a flat weight bench or Fitness Ball with both arms (or alternate single arm raises). A neutral grip can also be used – see neutral grip shoulder press on page 167.

Seated Shoulder Press

Start   Midpoint

Instruction

- Sit tall at the end of a flat weight bench with knees bent and feet resting on the ground and arms bent and raised at the side of body at shoulder height with palms facing forwards.
- Apply 3B's Principle™ - Brace, Breath and Body Position.
- Breathe out as you raise both dumbbells up overhead and in together with ends coming close together.
- Breathe in and lower back to shoulder height to complete one repetition.

Note: This exercise can also be performed standing, kneeling or sitting on a Fitness Ball with both arms (or alternate single arm raises). A neutral grip can also be used – see neutral grip shoulder press on page 167.

Fitness Ball Shoulder Press

Start   Midpoint

Instruction

- Sit tall on middle of Fitness Ball with knees bent and feet resting on the ground at shoulder-width and arms bent and raised at the side of body at shoulder height with palms facing forwards.
- Apply 3B's Principle™ - Brace, Breath and Body Position.
- Breathe out as you raise both dumbbells up overhead and in together with ends coming close together.
- Breathe in and lower back to shoulder height to complete one repetition.

Note: This exercise can also be performed standing with feet shoulder-width or in a forward lunge stance, kneeling or sitting on a flat weight bench with both arms or a single alternate arm raise – one arm at a time. A neutral grip can also be used – see neutral grip shoulder press on page 167.

Start

Right Arm

Left Arm

Dumbbell 2+1 Military Press

Instruction

- Sit tall at the end of a flat weight bench with knees bent and feet resting on the ground and arms bent and raised at the side of body at shoulder height with palms facing forwards.
- Apply 3B's Principle™ - Brace, Breath and Body Position.
- Breathe out as you raise the right arm up overhead.
- Breathe in as lower right arm back to shoulder height to complete one repetition.
- Breathe out as you raise the left arm up overhead.
- Breathe in as lower left arm back to shoulder height to complete the next repetition.

Note: The upwards movement can also be performed simultaneously – as one arm goes up the other lowers – in a standing, kneeling or seated position on a Fitness Ball. A neutral grip can also be used – see neutral grip shoulder press on page 167.

Neutral Grip Shoulder Press

Start   Midpoint

Instruction

- Stand tall with feet shoulder-width apart and arms bent and raised at the side of body at shoulder height with elbows tucked in close to the body and palms facing forwards.
- Apply 3B's Principle™ - Brace, Breath and Body Position.
- Breathe out as you raise both dumbbells straight up overhead keeping palms facing together.
- Breathe in and lower back to shoulder height to complete one repetition.

Note: This exercise can also be performed sitting on a flat weight bench or Fitness Ball or standing in a forward lunge stance. In addition a single alternate arm raise can also be performed – one arm at a time. See Functional progression in Stage 2.

Seated Arnold Shoulder Press

Start   Midpoint

Instruction

* Sit tall at the end of a flat weight bench with knees bent and feet resting on the ground and arms bent and held in front of the body close to the chest with palms facing inwards.
* Apply 3B's Principle™ - Brace, Breath and Body Position.
* Breathe out as you raise and rotate both dumbbells up and inwards overhead until palms are facing forwards – thumbs inwards.
* Breathe in and lower dumbbells back to chest in reverse motion to complete one repetition.

Note: This exercise can also be performed standing, kneeling or sitting on a Fitness Ball.

Lateral Raise

Start | Midpoint

Instruction
- Start in an upright standing position with feet shoulder-width apart and arms extended down by your side gripping dumbbells – knuckles facing outwards.
- Apply 3B's Principle™ - Brace, Breath and Body Position.
- Breathe out as you raise the arms out and up to the side in a semi-circular motion until arms are parallel to the ground – keeping wrists straight at all times and avoiding any forward head movement.
- Breathe in and lower to complete one repetition.

Note: This exercise can also be performed with the hands starting in front of the body and arms slightly bent – although this targets more of the anterior and medial deltoid, where the straight arm movement from the side of body focuses on the medial deltoid portion. The lateral raise itself can also be performed in a seated position on a flat weight bench or Fitness Ball or kneeling on the ground.

Seated Lateral Raise

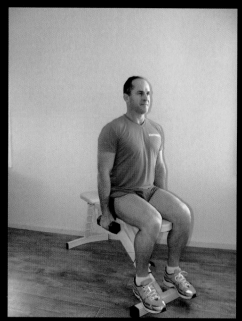

| Start | Midpoint |

Instruction
- Sit on end of flat weight bench with feet shoulder-width apart and arms extended down by your side gripping dumbbells – knuckles facing outwards.
- Apply 3B's Principle™ - Brace, Breath and Body Position.
- Breathe out as you raise the arms out and up to the side in a semi-circular motion until arms are parallel to the ground – keeping wrists and arms straight at all times and avoiding any forward head movement.
- Breathe in and lower to complete one repetition.

Note: This exercise can also be performed standing, kneeling or sitting on a Fitness Ball.

Single Arm Lateral Raise

Start   Midpoint

Instruction

- Start in an upright standing position with feet shoulder-width apart, one arm extended down by side of body gripping dumbbell – knuckles facing outwards – and the other arm gripping a bench for support.
- Apply 3B's Principle™ - Brace, Breath and Body Position.
- Breathe out as you raise the dumbbell out and up to the side in a semi-circular motion until arm is parallel to the ground – keeping wrists straight at all times and avoiding any forward head movement.
- Breathe in and lower to complete one repetition.
- Complete set and repeat with opposite arm.

Note: The single arm movement aims to reduce any forward head movement or neck tension through better focus and body control in strengthening the deltoid muscle.

Upright Rows – Wide Grip

Start · Midpoint

Instruction

- Start in an upright standing position with feet shoulder-width apart and arms extended down and wide outside of hip gripping dumbbells – knuckles facing forwards.
- Apply 3B's Principle™ - Brace, Breath and Body Position.
- Leading with the elbows, breathe out as you raise the elbows up high out wide until arms reach a 90-degree angle with upper arms parallel to the ground.
- Avoid any forward raising of the dumbbells or bending of the wrists.
- Breathe in and lower to complete one repetition.

Note: This movement is shorter in movement range than the close grip rows due to the wider angle and targeting medial deltoid.

See Stage 2: Functional Exercises for additional shoulder exercises including rotator cuff drills and combination exercises.

CHAPTER 4
STAGE 2: FUNCTIONAL EXERCISES

Stage 2:
Functional Exercises

"Paul Collins' training approach is a step above any other as he combines a progressive strength and functional training approach right through to Olympic Lifting movement patterns for achieving optimal strength and performance gains for our players."
Phil Blake, Head Coach
Manly Rugby Union Club

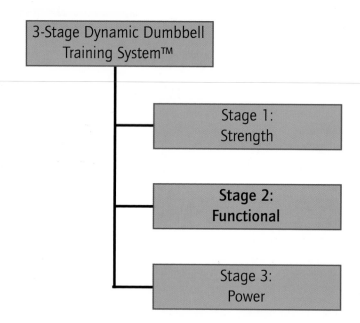

3-Stage Dynamic Dumbbell Training System™

Stage 1: Strength

Stage 2: Functional

Stage 3: Power

Balance Single Leg Rows

Start   Midpoint

Instruction

- Stand in a forward lunge position gripping dumbbells by your side – knuckles outwards.
- Bend at the hip and knee regions whilst leaning torso forwards until almost parallel to the ground. Raise the rear leg off ground keeping the hips square and arms extended down in front of body – knuckles outwards.
- Apply 3B's Principle™ - Brace, Breath and Body Position.
- Keep your head, neck, back and hips in neutral position at all times.
- Breathe out as you pull both arms up by bending at the elbows and raising high – keeping the arms close to the body.
- Breathe in as you lower the arms to complete one repetition.
- Complete set and repeat balancing on opposite leg.

This exercise targets the upper and lower back, abdominals, hip region and legs – requiring good stability, balance and core-control.

Three Set Sequence – Shrug, Upright Row, Curl

Starting Position   Shrug

Instruction

- Stand tall with feet hip-width apart gripping dumbbells at arm's length in front of thighs – knuckles facing forwards.
- Apply 3B's Principle™ - Brace, Breath and Body Position.
- Maintaining a constant breathing pattern perform the following sequence:
  - Shrug the shoulders up, then lower (shrug).
  - Raise the elbows up high to side until arms parallel to ground then lower (wide grip upright row).
  - Curl both arms up by bending elbows and raising dumbbells up to shoulder height with palms curling to face body, then lower bringing arms back in front of thigh again to complete one repetition.

This exercise targets the upper back, shoulders and biceps.

Upright Row

Biceps Curl

Rotator Cuff Drills

The following are a series of rotator cuff strengthening exercises often used in warming up the shoulder region or in rehabilitation of shoulder injuries. The best way to prevent a recurrence of injury is to strengthen your deeper shoulder muscles and keep them in peak condition through regular participation as part of a warm-up and warm-down routine. Prior to starting any exercises, always gain guidance and approval by your doctor or physical therapist for relative repetitions and sets.

ROTATOR CUFF STRENGTHENING EXERCISES

A. RESISTED EXTERNAL ROTATION

Lie on ground with upper arm bent at 90 degrees and dumbbell in hand. Rotate arm upwards away from your body and slowly return arm to starting position. Repeat on opposite arm, if necessary.

Perform 3 sets of 10-15 reps (or prior to fatigue)

Note: This exercise can also be performed lying on your back or standing (less resistance).

B. RESISTED INTERNAL ROTATION

Lie on ground with lower arm bent at 90 degrees and dumbbell in hand. Rotate arm upwards and in towards your body and slowly return arm to starting position. Repeat on opposite arm, if necessary.

Perform 3 sets of 10-15 reps (or prior to fatigue)

Note: This exercise can also be performed lying on your back or standing (less resistance).

C. RESISTED INTERNAL ROTATION IN ABDUCTION

Lie on ground with elbow inline with shoulder and arm bent at 90 degrees – dumbbell in hand. Rotate arm forwards until vertical then slowly return arm to starting position. Repeat on opposite arm, if necessary.

Perform 3 sets of 10-15 reps (or prior to fatigue)

Note: This exercise can also be performed standing for shoulder internal and external rotation in abduction.

D. RESISTED EXTERNAL ROTATION IN ABDUCTION

Lie across bench or chair with elbow inline with shoulder and arm bent at 90 degrees – dumbbell in hand. Rotate arm forwards until horizontal then slowly return arm to starting position. Repeat on opposite arm, if necessary.

Perform 3 sets of 10-15 reps (or prior to fatigue)

Note: This exercise can also be performed standing for shoulder internal and external rotation in abduction.

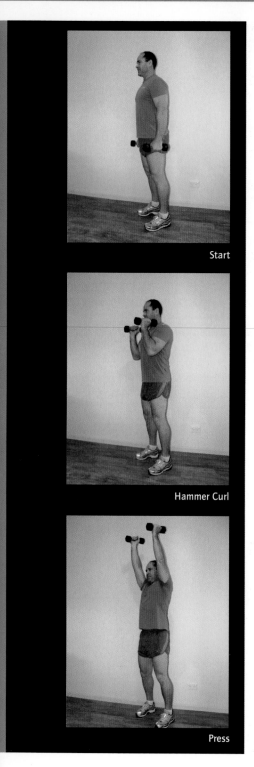

Start

Hammer Curl

Press

Hammer Curl and Press

Instruction

- Stand tall with feet hip-width apart gripping dumbbells at arm's length by your side – knuckles facing outwards.

- Apply 3B's Principle™ - Brace, Breath and Body Position.

- Maintain a deep breathing pattern as you bend and curl the arms, keeping elbows close to the body and raising hands up to shoulders performing a Hammer Curl with wrists remaining straight and knuckles outwards.

- From this position, push both arms straight up overhead, before bending the elbows and lowering dumbbells back to the shoulders then back down to your side to complete one repetition.

This exercise can also be performed in a seated position on a flat weight bench or Fitness Ball. It aims to strengthen the biceps and shoulder muscles with a focus on core control.

Squat Curls

Instruction

- Stand tall with feet hip-width apart gripping dumbbells at arm's length by your side – knuckles facing outwards.
- Apply 3B's Principle™ - Brace, Breath and Body Position.
- Breathe in as you simultaneously squat down until thighs parallel to the ground and curl the arms – bending at the hip, knees and ankles in the lower body and elbows of the upper body performing a Hammer Curl with wrists remaining straight and knuckles outwards.
- Breathe out as you rise up again returning to the starting position to complete one repetition.

This exercise aims to strengthen the biceps, glutes and legs with a focus on core control.

Start

Squat

Rise and Curl

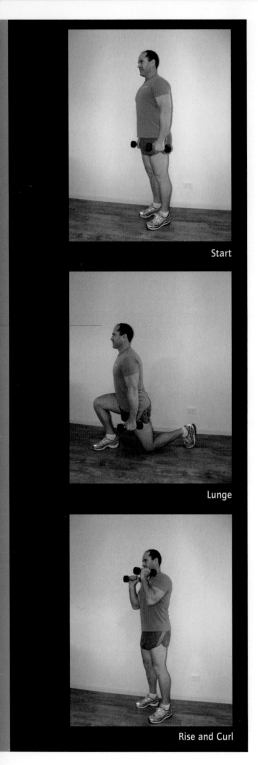

Start

Lunge

Rise and Curl

Dynamic Lunge and Curl

Instruction

- Stand tall with feet together gripping dumbbells at arms length by your side – knuckles facing outwards.
- Apply 3B's Principle™ - Brace, Breath and Body Position.
- Breathe in as you lunge forward with your left leg bending the front knee until thigh parallel whilst lowering rear knee towards ground.
- Breathe out as you push back up off the left leg to upright starting position whilst curling both arms performing a Hammer Curl with wrists remaining straight and knuckles outwards to complete one repetition.
- Repeat forward lunge movement and curl with right leg.

Note: This exercise can also be performed in a forward motion, continually lunging forwards for 8-15 steps or more. This exercise aims to strengthen the glutes, hamstrings, legs and biceps with a focus on core control.

Dynamic Lunge Rotation

Start   Midpoint

Instruction
- Stand tall with feet together gripping a single dumbbell at both ends, held parallel to ground with slightly bent arms at waist height in front of body – knuckles facing outwards.
- Apply 3B's Principle™ - Brace, Breath and Body Position.
- Breathe in as you simultaneously lunge forward with your left leg – bending the front knee until thigh parallel to ground with knees aligned over toes and rear knee lowered towards ground – whilst rotating dumbbell across to the left side of body and head remaining forwards.
- Breathe out as you push back up off the left leg and return legs and arms to the upright starting position to complete one repetition.
- Repeat forward lunge rotation with right leg.

Note: This exercise can also be performed in a forward motion, continually lunging forwards for 8-15 steps or more whilst rotating arms across the body. To add additional intensity to the exercise, lift the knee high and land forward with good body control. This exercise aims to strengthen the glutes, hamstrings, legs and abdominals with a focus on core control.

Lunge Press – A

Start   Midpoint

A = Single Dumbbell – both hands

Instruction
- Stand tall with feet together and single dumbbell held horizontally between both hands and resting in front of body at chest height.
- Apply 3B's Principle™ - Brace, Breath and Body Position.
- Breathing in, simultaneously raise arms up overhead whilst stepping forwards with one leg into a lunge position – front thigh is parallel to the ground and knee over toes.
- Breathe out as you rise back up to starting position and return arms to rest dumbbells again at chest height to complete one repetition.
- Repeat drill with opposite leg lunging forward.

Variation: This exercise can also be performed with both hands above head at all times or in a constant forward walking lunge movement pattern. This exercise aims to strengthen the glutes, hamstrings, legs and shoulders with a focus on core control.

Lunge Press – B

Start	Midpoint

B = Dumbbells in both hands

Instruction
- Stand tall with feet together and dumbbells resting in front of body at shoulder height.
- Apply 3B's Principle™ - Brace, Breath and Body Position.
- Breathing in, simultaneously raise arms up overhead whilst stepping forwards with one leg into a lunge position – front thigh is parallel to the ground and knee over toes.
- Breathe out as you rise back up to starting position and return arms to rest dumbbells again at shoulder height to complete one repetition.
- Repeat drill with opposite leg lunging forward.

Variation: This exercise can also be performed with both hands above head at all times or in a constant forward walking lunge movement pattern. This exercise aims to strengthen the glutes, hamstrings, legs and shoulders with a focus on core control.

Lunge Press – C

Start   Midpoint

C = Single dumbbell in one hand

Instruction
- Stand tall with feet together and single dumbbell held in right hand at shoulder height – knuckles facing outwards.
- Apply 3B's Principle™ - Brace, Breath and Body Position.
- Breathing in, simultaneously raise right arm up overhead whilst stepping forwards with right leg into a lunge position – front thigh is parallel to the ground and knee over toes.
- Breathe out as you rise back up to starting position and return arm to rest dumbbell again at shoulder height to complete one repetition.
- Repeat drill with opposite arm and leg.

Variation: Opposite Leg and Arm – Raise right arm as you lunge left leg forward and visa versa. In addition, this exercise can also be performed in a constant forward walking lunge movement pattern. To add additional intensity to the exercise lift the knee high and land forward with good body control or raise the free arm up to the side parallel to the ground. This exercise aims to strengthen the glutes, hamstrings, legs and shoulders with a focus on core control.

Lateral Lunge Press

Start   Midpoint

Instruction

- Stand tall with feet hip-width apart gripping dumbbells at shoulder height with arms ben
  and held close to body – knuckles facing outwards.
- Apply 3B's Principle™ - Brace, Breath and Body Position.
- Breathe in as you lunge out to one side – bending the front knee until thigh parallel tc
  ground with knees aligned over toes and rear leg straight – whilst pressing both arms up
  overhead with knuckles remaining facing outwards.
- Breathe out as you push back up off the forward leg and return legs and arms back to the
  upright starting position to complete one repetition.

Note: This exercise aims to strengthen the glutes, legs, shoulders and triceps with a focus or
core control. This exercise may also be performed using a biceps curl or lateral arm raises wher
lunging.

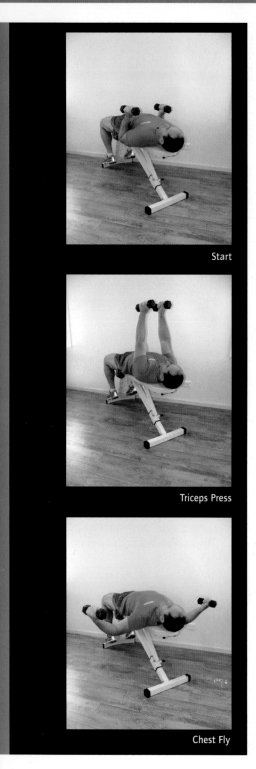

Start

Triceps Press

Chest Fly

Triceps Press and Chest Fly

Instruction

- Lie on back on flat weight bench with knees bent and feet on the ground shoulder-width apart and arms bent close to the body at chest height with knuckles facing outwards.

- Apply 3B's Principle™ - Brace, Breath and Body Position.

- Breathe out as you press both arms directly upwards to full extension – keeping straight wrists and knuckles outwards.

- From top end, breathe in as you lower arms out wide in a semi-circular motion bringing slight bend to the arms whilst lowering arms down to chest height.

- Breathe out again as you raise arms back up again in a semi-circular motion, keeping arms slightly bent at all times, until palms come together overhead.

- Breathe in and lower arms directly downwards back to your chest to complete one repetition.

This exercise targets the chest and triceps muscles.

Push-up Raise

Instruction

- Grip hexagon dumbbells in front support push-up position with arms extended and shoulders directly over hands – knuckles facing outwards – and body straight resting on toes 4 inches apart.
- Apply 3B's Principle™ - Brace, Breath and Body Position.
- Keep your head, neck and back in neutral position at all times.
- Breathe in as you lower chest towards hands keeping elbows close to the body.
- Breathe out and raise arms up whilst extending the right arm out to the side in a semi-circular motion until vertical through twisting of the body and maintaining a strong core. Once arm is extended overhead, lower it back down to upright starting position to complete one repetition.
- Repeat movement taking opposite arm overhead.

This exercise targets the chest, triceps, shoulders and core muscles.

Lower

Midpoint

Raise Arm

Single Arm Chest Press

Start   Midpoint

Instruction

- Lie on back and shoulders on Fitness Ball with feet resting on ground for support shoulder-width apart and one arm extended vertically, holding dumbbell – palms upwards, shoulder raised with dumbbell over eye-line – and the other arm bent and resting by shoulder.
- Apply the 3B's Principle™ - Brace, Breath and Body Position.
- Breathe in as you lower dumbbell by bending the elbow until the dumbbell is level with your chest – ensuring your core is held strong and extending the free arm up overhead for balance.
- Breathe out as you press the dumbbell back up overhead rolling shoulders slightly across ball and raised whilst returning the unweighted arm back by your side at shoulder level to complete one repetition.
- Complete set and repeat with opposite arm.

This exercise targets the chest and triceps and core control.

Alternate Arm Chest Press

Instruction

- Lie on back and shoulders on Fitness Ball with feet resting on ground for support shoulder-width apart and both arms extended up overhead – palms forwards.
- Apply the 3B's Principle™ - Brace, Breath and Body Position.
- Breathe out as you lower the right dumbbell down to shoulder height – keeping the opposite arm in starting position for balance.
- Breathe in as you raise the right arm back up to starting position to complete one repetition.
- Pause briefly and repeat lowering left arm, then back up.

This exercise targets the chest and triceps and core control. For variation, use an alternate sequence of lowering one arm whilst simultaneously raising the other.

Start

Right Arm Press

Left Raise Press

Single Leg Lateral Raise

Start   Midpoint

Instruction

- Stand tall on one leg, the other bent behind body, gripping dumbbells in front of body – knuckles outwards.
- Apply 3B's Principle™ - Brace, Breath and Body Position.
- Breathe out as you raise both arms up out wide to the side in a semi-circular motion until parallel to the ground – keeping wrists straight at all times.
- Breathe in as you lower the arms back to the side of body to complete one repetition.
- Complete set and repeat exercise balancing on opposite leg.

This exercise targets the shoulders, hip and core-control.

Lateral Lunge Raises

Instruction

- Stand tall with feet hip-width apart gripping dumbbells at arm's length by your side – knuckles facing outwards.
- Apply 3B's Principle™ - Brace, Breath and Body Position.
- Breathe in as you simultaneously lunge forward with your left leg – bending the front knee until thigh is parallel to the ground with knees aligned over toes and rear knee lowered towards ground – whilst laterally raising both arms to the side until parallel to the ground.
- Breathe out as you push back up off the left leg and return legs and arms to the upright starting position to complete one repetition.
- Repeat forward lunge with right leg and arms raised laterally.

This exercise targets the glutes, hamstrings, legs, shoulders and core-control.

Start

Lunge Raise

Return

Squat Lunge

Starting Position   Squat

Instruction

- Stand tall with feet hip-width apart gripping dumbbells at arm's length by your side – knuckles facing outwards.
- Apply 3B's Principle™ - Brace, Breath and Body Position.
- Breathe in as you squat until thighs are parallel by pushing back through the hips, knee and ankles.
- Breathe out as you rise up to starting position.
- Breathe in again as you lunge forward with your left leg – bending the front knee until thigh parallel to ground with knees aligned over toes and rear knee lowered towards ground – arms remain by your side.
- Breathe out as you push back up off the left leg and return body back up to the upright starting position to complete one repetition.
- Repeat squat and forward lunge with right leg.

Raised Position   Lunge and return

This exercise targets the glutes, thighs, hamstrings, legs and core-control. It can also be performed with the arms held in the following positions:

- Bent arms with dumbbells held in front of chest.
- Arms held isometrically at arm's length laterally and parallel to the ground.
- Arms extended overhead in Hammer Grip position – advanced level only.

Note: See additional arm positioning options on page 128.

Left leg lunge

Walk forwards

Right leg lunge

Walking Lunge

Instruction

- Stand tall with feet close together gripping dumbbells at arms length by your side – knuckles facing outwards.
- Apply 3B's Principle™ - Brace, Breath and Body Position.
- Breathe in as you lunge forward with your left leg – bending the front knee until thigh parallel to ground with knees aligned over toes and rear knee lowered towards ground – arms remain by your side.
- Breathe out as you continue in a forward motion lunging forward with your right leg with same action as prescribed above.
- Continue forwards for set distance or steps.
- To increase intensity through muscle control, raise knee high when lunging forwards – requiring more control when landing. Also see hand and arm position below.

This exercise targets the glutes, thighs, hamstrings, legs and core-control. It can also be performed with the arms held in the following positions:

- Bent arms with dumbbells held in front of chest.
- Arms held isometrically at arm's length laterally and parallel to the ground.
- Arms extended overhead – advanced level only.
- Arms pushing up overhead when lunging forwards.

Note: See additional arm positioning options on page 128.

Squat Jumps

Instruction

- Stand tall with feet hip-width apart gripping dumbbells at arm's length by your side – knuckles facing outwards.
- Apply 3B's Principle™ - Brace, Breath and Body Position.
- Breathe in as you simultaneously squat down until thighs parallel to the ground – bending at the hip, knees and ankles whilst keeping arms extended down by your side.
- Breathe out and drive upwards explosively through the legs – extending the legs and body vertically up off the ground then landing absorbing the force through controlled absorption in squat position.
- This movement can be performed repetitively for a set amount of jumps or through one jump, landing and re-setting before jumping again for a set amount of jumps also.

This exercise targets the lower body with a focus on explosive jump and core control.

Note: See additional arm positioning options on page 128.

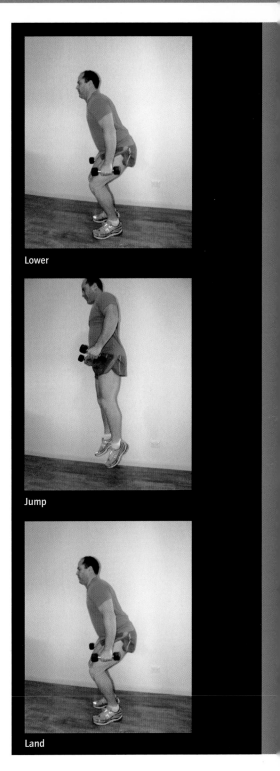

Lower

Jump

Land

197

Start

Lunge Forwards

Lunge Diagonal

Multi-Directional Lunge Sequence

Instruction

- Set up a series of 5 markers in a semi-circular arch one-lunge step away from body.
- Stand tall with feet close together gripping dumbbells at arms length by your side – knuckles facing outwards.
- Apply 3B's Principle™ - Brace, Breath and Body Position.
- Breathe in as you lunge forward with your left leg – bending the front knee until thigh is parallel to ground with knees aligned over toes and rear knee lowered towards ground – arms remain by your side.
- Breathe out as you push back off forward leg to the upright starting position.
- Repeat movement as follows:
  - Forwards and back.
  - 45-degree angle (diagonally) turning rear foot to face direction and back.
  - Sideways with rear leg straight and foot flat on ground and back.
  - Backwards diagonally at 45-degrees and back.
  - Backwards and back up to starting position.
- Repeat movement with right leg also.
- The hips should remain square at all times as well as maintaining good neutral pelvic control.

The lunge is a key movement pattern used in all sports and daily activities in movement and force generation. These lunges are assessed for stability at the hip, knee and ankle and for the participant's ability to coordinate and balance the movement. Lunges must be square with no wobbling or loss of form in the lunge and return phases on each leg.

Additional movements can be added to this exercise such as performing an arm curl or overhead press to increase the intensity.

Note: See additional arm positioning options on page 128.

Lunge to side

Lunge back diagonally

Lunge Backwards

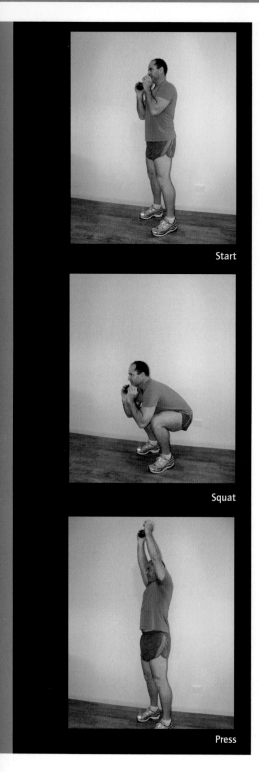

Start

Squat

Press

Single Dumbbell Squat Press

Instruction

- Stand tall with feet shoulder-width apart and arms bent in front of body holding a single dumbbell in both hands on each end at chest height.
- Apply 3B's Principle™ - Brace, Breath and Body Position.
- Breathe in as you simultaneously squat down until thighs parallel to the ground – bending at the hip, knees and ankles whilst keeping dumbbell against chest.
- Breathe out as you raise upwards whilst simultaneously extending dumbbell up overhead.
- Breathe in again as you lower arms and body back down into squat position – dumbbell against chest – to complete one repetition.

This exercise can also include using two dumbbells held in front of body at shoulder level and raised above head in same motion. This exercise targets the glutes, thighs, hamstrings, legs as well as the shoulders and abdominal muscles through core-control.

Push Press – Hammer Grip

Instruction

- Stand tall with feet shoulder-width apart and arms bent and tucked in close to chest hands and elbows parallel apart with dumbbells resting at shoulder height – knuckles facing outwards.
- Apply 3B's Principle™ - Brace, Breath and Body Position.
- Breathe in as you simultaneously dip at the hips, knees and ankles whilst keeping dumbbells in starting position before rapidly extending the arms and legs upwards vertically with dumbbells raising overhead – knuckles remaining outwards whilst breathing out.
- Breathe out as you raise upwards whilst simultaneously extending dumbbell up overheads to full extension.
- Breathe in again as you lower arms and dip at hips, knees and ankles to complete one repetition.

This exercise can also be performed with arms bent and raised out beside the body holding dumbbells at shoulder height – palms facing forwards. This exercise targets the glutes, legs and shoulders through core-control.

Start

Dip

Press

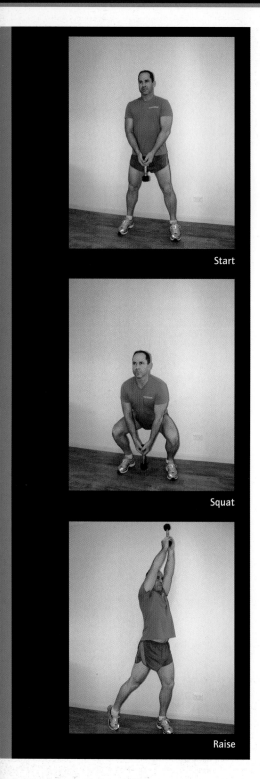

Start

Squat

Raise

Hay Bayler

Instruction

- Stand tall with feet wider than shoulder-width apart gripping a single dumbbell in both hands in front of body at waist height – both hands overlapped on dumbbell handle.
- Apply 3B's Principle™ - Brace, Breath and Body Position.
- Breathe in as you squat until thighs are parallel by pushing back through the hips, knee and ankles – lowering dumbbell between legs.
- Breathe out as you rise up raising dumbbell diagonally up and across the body to the left above the head and shoulder whilst extending up onto the ball of right foot and rotating through core of body to complete one repetition.
- Complete set and repeat movement with dumbbell in opposite direction raised diagonally across body.

This exercise targets the glutes, thighs, hamstrings, legs and abdominal oblique muscles through core-control and coordination.

CHAPTER 5

STAGE 3: POWER

Stage 3: Power

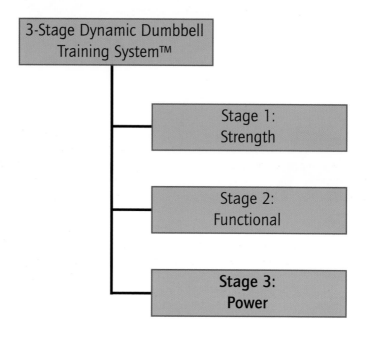

Exercise Progression and Technique

Stage 3 Power training provides a series of Olympic Lifting-based exercise drills using dumbbells that help establish strength, speed and technique that ultimately lead to developing explosive power and control. In this stage, a rapid development of force contributes to the development of further speed and power whilst gradually acclimatizing the Central Nervous System (CNS). As described in the Foundational Strength Training Zones chart, good technique is the first priority, using lighter dumbbells, prior to increasing the weight and more explosive movement.

It is much easier to have an athlete learn the lifting progressions in order to coordinate, master and perform the movement pattern before you put it all together with more advanced Olympic Lifts using dumbbells. This vital approach helps speeds up the learning curve and makes certain that the athlete establishes good technique, neuromuscular coordination and power. The progression element is critically important because along the way your body will have improved its core-strength and mobility and neuromuscular capacity. You will have also exposed the connective tissues, tendons, ligaments and muscle fibers to various angles and degrees of resistance and speed which helps the body become more functional in sport, allowing it to cope with a variety of forces and activities, whilst also reducing one's risk of injury.

As more complex dumbbell exercises are introduced, you'll feel a greater demand by the Central Nervous System (CNS) in performing each exercise. The strength gains from previous training stages are now being placed through a conversion process where a higher power output is required. The exercises themselves are becoming more complex and sports-specific in many ways.

Developing Explosive Power

To perform the lifts encountered in this chapter, you will have successfully progressed through training stages 1 and 2. When learning Olympic Lifts using dumbbells, it is essential that a major emphasis is placed on learning proper technique first using lighter weights. The goal is to increase power output which comes from moving a weight quickly. If the weight is too heavy, the dumbbells will move slowly and the athlete's technique will suffer potentially causing injury. Over time as technique and speed improves, gradually the dumbbell weight is increased that will contribute to effective development of speed and power conversion.

As a coach, I understand the importance and benefits of Olympic Lifting and the carry-over to one's sport, through better coordination and developing a higher rate of force. Even if that ranges from the traditional power clean to the much more complex snatch, Olympic Lifts train the athlete to explode and use the maximum possible force. As a result, quality of movement is favored over quantity with longer rest breaks to ensure the body is fresh when performing lifts.

Power Output Stages

Upon reaching this point in strength training, we see a rapid increase in the power output incurred in each lift. This requires a two-phase approach:

- **Power Phase 1:** light load (or weight) being lifted at high speed including medicine balls and Olympic Lifts; ensuring mastery of technique; lift speed often used to imitate sport specific power performed at high velocity such as the Shot Putt.

- **Power Phase 2:** heavy load being lifted at high speed.

Because of the rapid movements and muscle recruitment of these powerful lifts, the neural system is highly taxed requiring longer recovery periods between sets of between 3-5 minutes. In between sets, light cardiovascular exercise (i.e. stationary bike) can be performed to assist in feeding oxygen to the working muscles whilst also assisting later in the cooling down phase followed by stretching to reduce any muscle soreness.

Olympic Lifting Stretching Routine

Olympic Lifting requires tremendous strength, mobility and stability of a joint to ensure correct movement technique is maintained at all times. On some occasions, special attention may need to be applied regularly to ensure this mobility is maintained. The following stretches target specific muscular groups utilized in Olympic Lifts. Each stretch is held for up to 15 seconds or more and is repeated on both sides of the body, as required. Meanwhile, for those with excessive range of motion in one joint or a series of joints (commonly referred to as hypermobility) a stability-based approach is required, as opposed to stretching, for better muscle control.

Key Stretches	**Description**

Back extension – elbows
Objective: Stretch lower back muscles, to assist with set-up and first pull phases.

Lie on ground on stomach and forearms and gently raise chest up off ground and hold without stress or pain.

Chest stretch
Objective: Stretch chest muscles and assist in good body alignment, pulling movement and dumbbell position, especially when overhead.

Stand between door frame (or corner of two walls – L-shape) with arms at 90 degrees and gently lean forwards.

Mid-Back Arch
Objective: Stretch mid and upper back and shoulder region to assist with the dumbbell position, especially when overhead.

Stand opposite to wall and between door frame (or corner of two walls – L-shape). Bend at hips, place hands on wall and gently lean forwards.

Triceps
Objective: Stretch upper back, scapula and triceps important in shoulder and scapula mobility in all upper body and overhead movements.

Bend arms behind head and grip elbow with opposite hand. Gently pull downwards. Repeat with opposite arm.

Adductors
Objective: Stretch groin region to assist with rapid leg movement from bent to raised position.

Sit on ground with soles of feet together and place forearms along legs, gripping ankles with hands. Gently push knees down towards grounds by using your arms, before relaxing.

Hamstrings
Objective: Stretch hamstrings muscles involved in squat and lunge movements.

Sit on ground with legs extended and one foot on top of the other. Extend arms behind the body with fingers cupped and pointed. Keeping spine long gently lean forwards for stretch. Repeat with opposite leg.

Hip and Thoracic
Objective: Stretch hip and mid back region to ensure pliability of muscle for all movements.

Sit on ground with soles of feet together and place forearms along legs, gripping ankles with hands. Gently push knees down towards grounds by using your arms, before relaxing.

Lumbar rotation
Objective: Stretch hip, lower and mid back regions to ensure pliability of muscle for all movements.

Lie on ground with arms out wide and one leg bent across the other. Lower leg to side and face head across to other side. Repeat opposite direction.

Piriformis
Objective: Stretch deep gluteal muscles involved in all lower body movements.

From the above stretch, lean back onto ground and reach hand of bent leg through hole between legs and the other around outside of leg to both be placed just below knee and pull body close. Repeat opposite leg.

Standing Thigh
Objective: Stretch thigh muscles involved in all squat, lunge and lower body movements.

Standing tall grab foot and bend up behind body and hold. Repeat opposite leg.

Kneeling sacroiliac joint
Objective: Stretch deep gluteal muscles and sacroiliac joint involved in all lower body movements.

Kneel on ground and lean forwards onto forearms. Cross one leg behind the other keeping the hips square. Repeat opposite leg.

Kneeling hip flexors

Kneeling Side Reach
Objective: Stretch thigh muscles involved in all squat, lunge and lower body movements.

Standing tall, grab foot and bend up behind body and hold. Repeat with opposite leg.

Olympic Lifts

The following exercises are dynamic in nature and require adequate flexibility through the shoulder, back and hip regions to perform correctly. Always practice with light dumbbells first to improve technique and coordination. Apply the 3B's Principle™ - Brace, Breathe and Body Position as part of each Olympic Lift exercise to ensure good quality movement patterns and control at all times. Ensure an appropriate warm-up is undertaken. Always seek professional guidance and one-on-one coaching when undertaking any new exercise.

Single-Arm Olympic Lifts

Hang Position

Starting Position

Hang Position

The 'hang position' is a progressive starting movement of an Olympic Lift that can be utilized in addition to exercises prescribed in Stage 3, where appropriate. This entails starting in a tall standing position holding a dumbbell (or pair off dumbbells) in an extended position in front of waist or side of body. This is followed by a squat type movement – bending at hips, knees and ankles – whilst simultaneously lowering the arm forwards, slightly above or just below the knee, followed by the specific pull and/or clean and jerk action of an Olympic Lift.

The hang starting position illustrated above and exercise on the next page can be utilized as an added exercise version to many exercises in Stage 3. The dumbbell(s) position itself will vary depending on the specific exercise. Apply accordingly. Repeat exercise with opposite arm.

Single Arm Hang High Pull

Instruction

- Stand tall with the dumbbell extended down at thigh level.

- Lean forward at the hips with slight knee bend until the dumbbell hangs slightly above (or below) the knee – maintaining neutral curvature of the spine.

- Drive the body up through extension of the legs, thrusting the hips forward – keeping the dumbbell close to your body.

- As the lower body reaches full extension, shrug the shoulders and pull the dumbbell up towards the chest leading with the elbow whilst simultaneously rising up onto the toes.

Note: This exercise is an example of a Hang Start Position that can be utilized for many exercises in Stage 3. Apply accordingly. Repeat exercise with opposite arm.

Start

Hang

High Pull

Start

High Pull

Lower

Single Arm High Pull

Instruction

- Start in squat position with dumbbell by your side.
- Drive the body up through extension of the legs, thrusting the hips forward – keeping the dumbbell close to your body.
- Maintain the same torso angle during the initial pull phase avoiding the hips rising before or faster than the shoulders.
- Ensure the spine remains neutral and does not round while pulling the dumbbell.
- As the lower body reaches full extension, shrug the shoulders and pull the dumbbell up towards the chest leading with the elbow whilst simultaneously rising up onto the toes.
- Repeat exercise with opposite arm.

Single Arm Push Press

Instruction

- Start with the dumbbell at shoulder height tucked in close to the body, elbow forward in a rack position.
- Gently dip at hip and knees simultaneously before rapidly thrusting up vertically driving and locking the arm out directly above the head.
- Ensure that the dumbbell travels straight up and that the arm locks out at the top whilst keeping rigid through the torso and maintaining good body posture.
- Repeat exercise with opposite arm.

Start

Dip

Press

213

Start

Deep split

Finish

Single Arm Deep Jerk

Instruction

- Start with the dumbbell at shoulder height tucked in close to the body, elbow forward in a rack position.
- Gently dip simultaneously at hip and knees before rapidly thrusting up vertically jumping into a deep split stance position (with opposite leg to arm forward) – locking the arm out directly above the head.
- Ensure that the dumbbell travels straight up and that the arm locks out at the top whilst keeping rigid through the torso and maintaining good body posture.
- Once the dumbbell is stable above the head bring the feet back to a parallel stance.
- Repeat exercise with opposite arm.

Single Arm Hang Power Clean

Instruction

- Stand tall with the dumbbell extended down at thigh level.
- Lean forward at the hips with slight knee bend until the dumbbell hangs slightly below the knee – maintaining neutral curvature of the spine.
- Drive the body up through extension of the legs, thrusting the hips forward – keeping the dumbbell close to your body.
- As the dumbbell reaches near maximum height, rapidly flex the elbow to bring the body under the dumbbell (elbow tucked into the body and dumbbell at shoulder height in a rack position) lowering down into a semi-squat position then immediately stand up.
- Ensure the spine remains neutral and does not round while pulling the dumbbell.
- Repeat exercise with opposite arm.

Start

Pull

Catch

Start

Pull

Catch

Single Arm Power Clean

Instruction

- Start in squat position with dumbbell by your side.
- Drive the body up through extension of the legs, thrusting the hips forward – keeping the dumbbell close to your body.
- Maintain the same torso angle during the initial pull phase avoiding the hips rising before or faster than the shoulders.
- As the dumbbell reaches near maximum height rapidly flex the elbow to bring the body under the dumbbell (elbow tucked into the body and dumbbell at shoulder height in a rack position) lowering down into a semi-squat position then immediately stand up.
- Ensure the spine remains neutral and does not round while pulling the dumbbell.

Variation: See page 211 for application of Hang Start Position with this exercise. Repeat exercise with opposite arm.

Single Arm Clean

Instruction

- Start in squat position with dumbbell by your side.
- Drive the body up through extension of the legs, thrusting the hips forward – keeping the dumbbell close to your body.
- Maintain the same torso angle during the initial pull phase avoiding the hips rising before or faster than the shoulders.
- As the dumbbell reaches near maximum height, rapidly flex the elbow to bring the body under the dumbbell (elbow tucked into the body and dumbbell at shoulder height in a rack position) lowering down into a full front squat position then immediately stand up.
- Ensure the spine remains neutral and does not round while pulling the dumbbell.

Variation: See page 211 for application of Hang Start Position with this exercise. Repeat exercise with opposite arm.

Start

Pull

Catch and squat

Rise

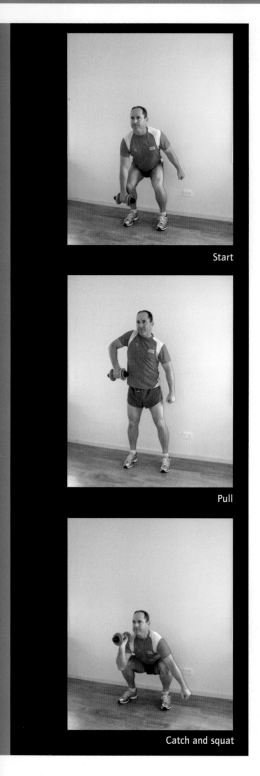

Start

Pull

Catch and squat

Single Arm Clean and Jerk

Instruction

- Start in squat position with dumbbell by your side.
- Drive the body up through extension of the legs, thrusting the hips forward – keeping the dumbbell close to your body.
- Maintain the same torso angle during the initial pull phase avoiding the hips rising before or faster than the shoulders.
- Ensure the spine remains neutral and does not round while pulling the dumbbell.
- Repeat exercise with opposite arm.

- As the dumbbell reaches near maximum height, rapidly flex the elbow to bring the body under the dumbbell (elbow tucked into the body and dumbbell at shoulder height in a rack position) lowering down into a full front squat position then immediately stand up.

- From the standing rack position, briefly dip body and thrust arm and body up rapidly into split leg stance position (with opposite leg to arm forward) whilst locking the arm out above the head.

- When the dumbbell is stable above the head, bring the feet to a parallel stance.

Variation: See page 211 for application of Hang Start Position with this exercise. Repeat exercise with opposite arm.

Rise

Dip and Split Stance

Finish

Start

Squat and Jerk

Finish

Single Arm Push Jerk

Instruction

- Start with the dumbbell at shoulder height tucked in close to the body, elbow forward in a rack position.
- Allow a brief dip at hip and knees before rapidly driving arm up overhead to lock out and lowering your body down into full squat position, then stand up.
- Ensure the arm remains locked directly overhead when lowering and raising the body.
- Upon initial explosive movement, you may jump your feet slightly wider to allow for a more effective movement pattern and body control.
- Repeat exercise with opposite arm.

Single Arm Power Snatch

Instruction

- Start in squat position with arm holding dumbbell extended down inside legs.

- Drive the body up through extension of the legs, thrusting the hips forward – keeping the dumbbell close to your body.

- Maintain the same torso angle during the initial pull phase avoiding the hips rising before or faster than the shoulders.

- Ensure the spine remains neutral and does not round while pulling the dumbbell.

- As the dumbbell reaches near maximum height, rapidly extend the elbow to bring the body under the dumbbell as the arm extends and locks overhead.

Variation: See page 211 for application of Hang Start Position with this exercise. Repeat exercise with opposite arm.

Start

Pull

Finish

Single Arm Snatch

Start

Pull

Instruction

- Start in squat position with arm holding dumbbell extended down inside legs.
- Drive the body up through extension of the legs, thrusting the hips forward – keeping the dumbbell close to your body.
- Maintain the same torso angle during the initial pull phase avoiding the hips rising before or faster than the shoulders.
- Ensure the spine remains neutral and does not round while pulling the dumbbell.
- As the dumbbell reaches near maximum height, rapidly extend the elbow to bring the body under the dumbbell overhead whilst locking the arm out and lowering your body down into full squat position, then stand up.

Variation: See page 211 for application of Hang Start Position with this exercise. Repeat exercise with opposite arm.

Squat

Finish

Double Arm Olympic Lifts

This section incorporates the use of two dumbbells simultaneously. The Hang Start Position, mentioned in Single Arm Olympic Lifts, can also be utilized with many of the following exercises.

Squat Shrug

Instruction

- Start in a squat position with arms extended down and dumbbells positioned outside line of the feet – maintaining neutral curvature of the spine.
- Drive the body up through extension of the legs, thrusting the hips forward – keeping the dumbbells close to your body.
- Shrug the shoulders when the lower body reaches full extension while trying to keep the arms straight.
- Ensure the spine remains neutral and does not round while pulling the dumbbells.

Variation: See page 211 for application of Hang Start Position with this exercise. Repeat exercise with opposite arm.

Start

Shrug

Finish

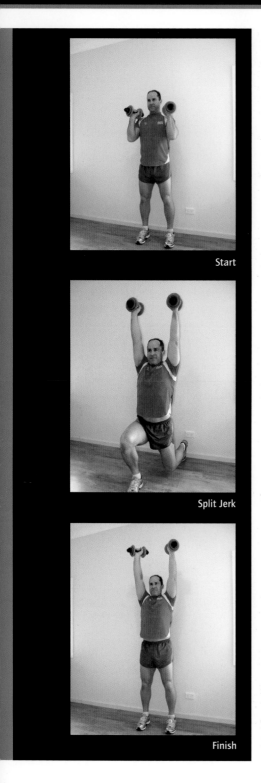

Start

Split Jerk

Finish

Deep Jerk

Instruction

- Start with the dumbbells at shoulder height with elbows tucked in close to the body in a rack position.

- Smoothly dip at hip and knees keeping the torso rigid and vertical before rapidly thrusting up vertically jumping into a deep split stance – locking the arms out directly above the head.

- Ensure that the dumbbells travel straight up and that the arm locks out at the top whilst keeping rigid through the torso and maintaining good body posture.

- Once the dumbbells are stable above the head along with good core control, bring the feet back to a parallel stance.

Note: A mid jerk position with less leg bend can also be utilized in the initial strengthening phases of one's development.

Deep Push Jerk

Instruction

- Start with the dumbbells at shoulder height with elbows tucked in close to the body in a rack position.
- Smoothly dip at the hip and knees keeping the torso rigid and vertical before rapidly thrusting body up onto toes, whilst simultaneously locking both arms out directly above the head and rapidly lowering into a full squat position before standing up.
- Ensure that the dumbbells travel straight up and that the arm locks out at the top whilst keeping rigid through the torso and maintaining good body posture throughout the whole movement.

Start

Squat

Finish

Start

Dip

Finish

Push Press

Instruction

- Start with the dumbbells at shoulder height with elbows tucked in close to the body in a rack position.
- Smoothly dip at the hip and knees keeping the torso rigid and vertical before rapidly thrusting body up and pushing arms up overhead into a locked position.
- Ensure that the dumbbells travel straight up and that the arm locks out at the top whilst keeping rigid through the torso and maintaining good body posture.

Power Clean

Instruction

- Start in a squat position with arms extended down and dumbbells positioned outside line of the feet – maintaining neutral curvature of the spine.
- Drive the body up through extension of the legs, thrusting the hips forward – keeping the dumbbells close to your body.
- Ensure the spine remains neutral and does not round while pulling the dumbbells.
- As the dumbbells reach near maximum height rapidly flex the elbow to bring the body under the dumbbells (elbows tucked into the body and dumbbells at shoulder height in a rack position) and lower down into a semi-squat position then immediately stand up.

Variation: See page 211 for application of Hang Start Position with this exercise.

Start

Pull

Catch

Power Clean and Press

Start   Pull

Instruction

- Start in a squat position with arms extended down and dumbbells positioned outside line of the feet – maintaining neutral curvature of the spine.
- Drive the body up through extension of the legs, thrusting the hips forward – keeping the dumbbell close to your body.
- Ensure the spine remains neutral and does not round while pulling the dumbbells.

Catch   Raise

- As the dumbbells reach near maximum height, rapidly flex the elbow to bring the body under the dumbbells (elbows tucked into the body and dumbbells at shoulder height in a rack position) and lower down into a semi-squat position then immediately stand up.
- From here, smoothly dip at the hip and knees keeping the torso rigid and then rapidly explode body upwards simultaneously thrusting both arms overhead.

Variation: See page 211 for application of Hang Start Position with this exercise.

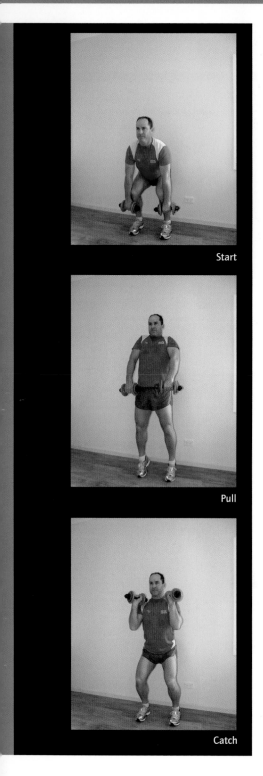

Start

Pull

Catch

Power Clean and Split Jerk

Instruction

- Start in a squat position with arms extended down and dumbbells positioned outside line of the feet – maintaining neutral curvature of the spine.
- Drive the body up through extension of the legs, thrusting the hips forward – keeping the dumbbell close to your body.
- Ensure the spine remains neutral and does not round while pulling the dumbbells.

- As the dumbbells reach near maximum height, rapidly flex the elbow to bring the body under the dumbbells (elbows tucked into the body and dumbbells at shoulder height in a rack position) and lower down into a semi-squat position, then immediately stand up.

- From here, smoothly dip at the hip and knees keeping the torso rigid and then rapidly explode body upwards into a split-stance position with arms extended and locked overhead. Split into deeper stance only when core control and strength improves.

- Once the dumbbells overhead are stable, along with good core control, bring the feet back to a parallel stance.

Variation: See page 211 for application of Hang Start Position with this exercise.

Rise

Split Stance

Finish

Start

Pull

Split Power Clean

Instruction

- Start in a squat position with arms extended down and dumbbells positioned outside line of the feet – maintaining neutral curvature of the spine.
- Drive the body up through extension of the legs, thrusting the hips forward – keeping the dumbbell close to your body.
- Ensure the spine remains neutral and does not round while pulling the dumbbells.
- As the dumbbells reach near maximum height, rapidly flex the elbow to bring the body under the dumbbells (elbows tucked into the body and dumbbells at shoulder height in a rack position) whilst jumping into a split-stance position before bringing the feet back to a parallel stance.
- As body control and strength improves, a deep split stance position can be introduced.

Variation: See page 211 for application of Hang Start Position with this exercise.

Split stance

Finish

Clean

Instruction

- Start in a squat position with arms extended down and dumbbells positioned outside line of the feet – maintaining neutral curvature of the spine.

- Drive the body up through extension of the legs, thrusting the hips forward – keeping the dumbbells close to your body.

- Ensure the spine remains neutral and does not round while pulling the dumbbells.

- As the dumbbells reach near maximum height, rapidly flex the elbow to bring the body under the dumbbells (elbows tucked into the body and dumbbells at shoulder height in a rack position) lowering down into a full-squat position then immediately stand up.

Variation: See page 211 for application of Hang Start Position with this exercise.

Start

Pull

Catch and squat

Finish

Start

Pull

Clean and Press

Instruction

- Start in a squat position with arms extended down and dumbbells positioned outside line of the feet – maintaining neutral curvature of the spine.

- Drive the body up through extension of the legs, thrusting the hips forward – keeping the dumbbell close to your body.

- Ensure the spine remains neutral and does not round while pulling the dumbbells.

- As the dumbbells reach near maximum height, rapidly flex the elbow to bring the body under the dumbbells (elbows tucked into the body and dumbbells at shoulder height in a rack position) and lower down into a full-squat position then immediately stand up extending both arms overhead into locked position.

Variation: See page 211 for application of Hang Start Position with this exercise.

Catch and Squat

Press

Clean and Jerk

Instruction

- Start in a squat position with arms extended down and dumbbells positioned outside line of the feet – maintaining neutral curvature of the spine.

- Drive the body up through extension of the legs, thrusting the hips forward – keeping the dumbbell close to your body.

- Ensure the spine remains neutral and does not round while pulling the dumbbells.

- As the dumbbells reach near maximum height rapidly flex the elbow to bring the body under the dumbbells (elbows tucked into the body and dumbbells at shoulder height in a rack position) and lower down into a full-squat position then immediately stand up.

- From here, smoothly dip at the hip and knees keeping the torso rigid and then rapidly explode body upwards into a split-stance position with arms extended and locked overhead. Split into deeper stance only when core control and strength improves.

- Once the dumbbells overhead are stable, along with good core control, bring the feet back to a parallel stance.

1. Start
2. Pull
3. Catch and Squat
4. Split stance
5. Finish

Variation: See page 211 for application of Hang Start Position with this exercise.

Start

Pull

Catch

Power Snatch

Instruction

- Start in a squat position with arms extended down and dumbbells positioned outside line of the feet – maintaining neutral curvature of the spine.

- Drive the body up through extension of the legs, thrusting the hips forward and rising up onto the toes pulling the dumbbells upward close to your body.

- As the dumbbells reach near maximum height, rapidly flex the elbow to bring the body under the dumbbells as the arms lock out overhead and the body lowers into a full-squat position, then immediately stand up.

Variation: See page 211 for application of Hang Start Position with this exercise.

Snatch

Instruction

- Start in a squat position with arms extended down and dumbbells positioned outside line of the feet – maintaining neutral curvature of the spine.

- Drive the body up through extension of the legs, thrusting the hips forward and rising up onto the toes pulling the dumbbells upward close to your body.

- As the dumbbells reach near maximum height, rapidly flex the elbow to bring the body under the dumbbells as the arms lock out overhead and the body lowers into a full-squat position, then immediately stand up.

Variation: See page 211 for application of Hang Start Position with this exercise.

Start

Pull

Catch and squat

Rise

CHAPTER 6
BONUS KETTLEBELL DRILLS

What is a Kettlebell?

A kettlebell is a heavy cast iron ball with a handle on it originating from Russia that is used for functional strength development in athletes and training variety for fitness enthusiasts.

The design of the kettlebell makes it unique because when you grip the handle, the weight is displaced differently when compared to that of a dumbbell – making you work harder to control the movement through counterbalance and grip control of the handle through different angles of movement.

Benefits of Kettlebell Training

Kettlebell training aims to develop strength through all planes of movement. Because the Kettlebell aligns with the body's center of gravity, the athlete must work harder to balance and stabilize the weight throughout all movement patterns. This requires a strong contribution from the muscles of the arm, shoulder and core region. Along with this comes improvement in strength, power and body awareness for better muscle control by addressing both acceleration and deceleration of movement. Best of all, the challenging nature of kettlebell training works the whole body making exercise fun and rewarding!

Safety Tips

Overuse

Care must be used when isolating specific muscles not to create an unbalanced condition. Unbalanced muscles may allow a particular muscle to work harder than the supporting and stabilizing muscles, thereby increasing the chances of injury. The aim is to create muscular balance by working all muscle groups as opposed to focusing on any single area.

No Pain Principle

If when exercising you feel any sharp or concerning pain, always stop the exercise immediately. Ensure you perform a proper warm-up before continuing. If pain persists, always seek medical advice straight away.

Kettlebell Variations

Different Kettlebell brands will vary in shape, weight, size and handle thickness. This is important to remember as it will often change the weight displacement and movement mechanics requiring a higher skill focus.

Choosing a Kettlebell Weight

When starting any new exercise or movement pattern, the kettlebell weight should be light and the technique mastered, before progressing to a heavier weight. This ensures the muscles, joints and connective tissues adapt to the demands of each exercise.

Static Strength before Dynamic Strength

With kettlebells it is very important to start with basic isolated movement patterns to build good core-strength and body awareness before introducing more dynamic functional multi-muscle – complex movement patterns. In other words, learn and perform simple movements before complex ones.

Hand Control

In most exercises, as the exercise movement occurs it requires periods where the handle itself swivels within the palm of the hand before a firm grip is applied. This requires good hand, wrist, elbow, arm and shoulder strength for movement control and essential core-strength to maintain balance.

Speed of Movement

The speed of movement at which each repetition is performed plays a vital role in Kettlebell training. Due to the weight displacement, movements need to first be learnt in a slow-controlled movement pattern using a light kettlebell to install essential muscle memory that can be drawn upon when advancing to more dynamic movements of a similar nature using a heavier kettlebell.

Kettlebell Key Movement Patterns

1. Hip Thrust Development

The hip thrust plays a major role in the kettlebell swing motion of the arms, and movement of the legs in a squat motion through pelvic control of the lower body region. In order to learn the required technique of snapping the hips forward and clasping the glutes whilst locking out the legs in any swinging motion, the following two exercises should be mastered before any swinging movement is introduced.

Hip Thrust Exercise 1: Hamstrings Bridge with pelvic thrust and glute clutching.

Lowered   Raised

Lying on your back, squeeze your glutes and tighten your abs as you raise up on your heels. Breathe out with exertion.

Hip Thrust Exercise 2 – Sumo Squat

Start with feet wider than shoulder-width apart
(1) Exhale upwards
(2) Push hips forwards and squeeze (clasp) butt cheeks
(3) Push feet into ground
(4) Ensure core is tight
(5) Inhale while lowering

Hip Thrust Exercise 3 – Muscle Control

Pressurize core by squeezing your glutes and tightening your abs when swinging kettlebell up from a squat position with the arms and locking the legs out. Avoid leaning backwards.

All movements utilizing a kettlebell require counter-balancing throughout the body for movement control. For instance, whilst swinging the kettlebell upwards with the arms and extending the hips forwards, the movement requires counter-balancing through the posterior muscles of the calf, hamstrings, gluteal and lower back regions. As the body extends, the hips are quickly snapped forwards whilst the gluteal muscles are squeezed together.

As the kettlebell swings back down between the legs, the abdominal core muscles need to be heavily contracted as an effective counterbalance mechanism.

Timing and proficiency between muscle groups in each movement is the vital ingredient for successful kettlebell training. Start with a light kettlebell and master this before progressing to a heavier one.

2. Rack Position

The rack position refers to the position of the arm in a starting position or when the kettlebell is raised to the chest from the ground and prior to overhead lifting. Variables of the rack position include an overhand grip in the following positions:

| 1. Palms to chest | 2. Knuckles to side |

Ensure shoulders are back and shoulders blades squeezed together – abdominals braced applying 3B's Principle™. The two different rack positions will depend on one's flexibility and muscle control.

3. Pick-up Position

Grip:
Both Hands – Knuckles forwards
Single Hand – Thumb facing slightly in and backwards

Starting Point:
A. Kettlebell in line with feet
B. Step forwards of kettlebell (behind heels) – then pick up

With these key movement patterns in mind, I have put together a number of general kettlebell exercises to get you started for an effective full body workout.

Stationary Lunge Cross-Overs

Start   Midpoint

Stand tall in an upright stationary lunge position with one hand holding kettlebell by your side. Descending into a lowered lunge position, switch kettlebell under leg into opposite hand and up and over leg as you rise back to starting position. Repeat movement for set amount of reps before changing legs.

Lunge Switch-Overs

Start | Midpoint

Stand tall with feet together holding kettlebell in one hand by your side. Lunge forwards with opposite leg to hand and switch kettlebell under leg before rising and repeating sequence on opposite side.

Figure 8's

Start

Stand in wide stance with kettlebell extended down in front of body held in one hand. Initiate movement by swinging the kettlebell back and across under opposite leg; looping under leg and swapping hands. Maintain a fluid motion as you loop the kettlebell over the leg and back to the center and across under the opposite leg repeating previous movement to form a figure 8 movement pattern, before squatting again and repeating for desired time or reps – only with good form.

Under

Loop

Across

Single Leg Deadlift

Start   Midpoint

Stand on one leg with opposite arm extended down holding kettlebell – knuckles outwards. Apply 3B's Principle™ - brace, breath, and body position. Keeping back flat and hips square, lower forwards until back is parallel to ground, then rise. Repeat drill on opposite side.

Single Leg Squat

Start   Midpoint

Stand on one leg with the other extended and hands holding kettlebell in front of the body. Breathing in, simultaneously bend the knee and lower body pushing the gluteus back whilst shoulders remain over knees, into squat position before rising. Vary depth to suit strength and stability levels. Repeat with opposite leg.

Double Arm Front Swing

Start   Midpoint

Stand in wide stance with kettlebell extended down in front of body held in both hands. Initiate movement by swinging the kettlebell backwards through legs, keeping the back flat and weight on heels, then up in front of body whilst rising, before squatting again and repeating for desired time or repetitons – only with good form.

Single Arm Front Swing

Start   Midpoint

Stand in wide stance with kettlebell extended down in front of body in one hand. Initiate movement by swinging the kettlebell backwards through legs, keeping the back flat and weight on heels, then up in front of body whilst rising, before squatting again and repeating for desired time or reps – only with good form. Repeat with opposite arm.

Front Swing Switch-Overs

Stand with your feet wider than shoulder-width, legs bent in squat position, back flat, head forwards and arms extended down gripping kettlebell with one hand – knuckles forwards. Apply 3B's Principle™ - brace, breath, and body position. Simultaneously rise up from squat position whilst swinging arm forwards. It may take you 2-3 swings to reach the required height of swing – arms above parallel. At the top of the arm movement swap hands as you tighten your abdominal muscles and glutes before lowering back down to squat position, maintaining good muscle control and sequencing at all times and repeating movement with opposite arm.

Start

Raise

Swap

Lower

Single Arm Squat Push Press

Start   Midpoint

Start with kettlebell in rack position. Descend by allowing the hips, knees and ankles to flex to half or full squat position while keeping the knees aligned over feet before rising and extending the arms overhead, then back to rack position. Repeat with opposite arm.

Get Ups

Lie on back with legs straight and left arm extended vertically holding kettlebell – palm upwards. Keeping the kettlebell arm locked out at all times, roll across onto your right arm triceps and up onto hand and right thigh. Keep watch of the kettlebell as you continue to push up on the right hand and knee, before rising up onto both feet with kettlebell raised vertically overhead. Take a moment to reset your body position before reversing the movement back down to the ground, maintaining full body control whilst watching the kettlebell and keeping arms locked out at all times. Repeat exercise holding kettlebell in opposite hand.

Lie on back

Roll

Knee

Stand

CHAPTER 7
PROGRAM DESIGN

Program Design

Strength Training Routines

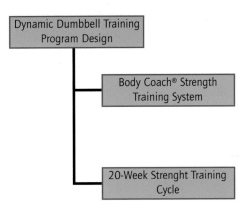

Strength training plays an important role in neuromuscular strength and coordination required for improvements in maximum strength, body shape improvement and optimal athletic performance. In this chapter I will provide you with a number of strength training programs for muscle gain, fat loss, sports and general fitness.

To ensure safe progress with strength training, adhere to the following Dynamic Dumbbell Training guidelines:

- Gain approval to exercise from your doctor, especially if you are pregnant or have a previous injury.
- See a physical therapist to assess your posture and joint mechanics and approve appropriate exercises for you.
- Get to know your muscles to understand their function.
- Have a strength and conditioning coach demonstrate each exercise and correct any faults you may have.
- Warm-up the body prior to exercising followed by pre-activity stretching
- Apply the 3B's Principle™ for helping maintaining correct body posture and maximize your training outcomes.
- Ensure the head and neck maintain a neutral position in line with the body at all times.
- If at any stage during exercising you feel tension, numbness, dizziness or pain, stop the exercise immediately and seek medical advice.
- Warm up with 5-10 minutes of low- to moderate-intensity cardiovascular exercise, light dumbbell movements and stretches for the whole body.
- Emphasize quality of movement over quantity.
- Rest 60–300 seconds between each set, as required.
- Drink at least 2 glasses of water during your workout, then afterwards.
- Give yourself at least 24-72 hours to recover before repeating for strength and power training, respectively, for the same muscle group.
- Cool down with light cardiovascular exercise and a gentle stretching routine after your workout.

Strength Training Starting Point

Sets and repetitions are the building blocks of your strength training routine. A repetition (or rep) is one complete execution of an exercise. So, for example, one rep of a squat exercise would be the full cycle squatting down and then back up. On the other hand, a set refers to a series of repetitions (i.e: 8 reps complete one set) followed by a recovery period. In scientific terms, a movement is often classified as eccentric (negative or down part) and concentric (positive or up part) such as that in a dumbbell bench press or squat exercise. I mention these terms because over time you will hear a number of words in the gym or readings used to describe an exercise or movement that have similar meaning. In our case, my aim is to keep things as simple as possible.

Each repetition should also move through its full range of motion. In the case of the dumbbell bench press exercise, this means pushing the weight up (concentric) until your arms are straight, then lowering it back down (eccentric) towards the chest without stopping. The specific number of sets and repetitions are determined by one's training objective as described previously in the **8 Key Elements, Progressive Resistance Training and the Foundation Strength Training Zone.**

A training cycle is generally applied in 4-week period intervals. For instance, the general preparation cycle may be performed over 4 weeks, before moving on to a hypertrophy strength training cycle for 4 weeks and so forth. As strength and muscle coordination improves during this 4-week period, a small increase in the maximal percentage of weight being lifted can be applied or a new exercise for the same muscle group introduced.

In advanced training, percentiles are calculated by performing a one repetition (1RM) maximum lift. But when first starting out, there is a period of 4-12 weeks where the body needs to adapt appropriately before these tests are undertaken – under the supervision of a qualified strength and conditioning coach. In the beginning, using a light weight that fulfills the required amount of reps will give you the starting point to build from as your knowledge and understanding increases. As the body adapts quickly and needs new variables, either the dumbbell weight being lifted is increased, the tempo is changed, the recovery period is reduced or a new exercise for the same muscle group is introduced.

In strength training terms, progressive resistance training would mean lifting a heavier weight once your body has adjusted to the usual weight lifted. It is wise to first increase the number of repetitions and sets rather than increase the weight. Only once you have increased the repetitions and sets should you then look for further gains by increasing the weight. With repetition changes throughout the program – for example – from 10 to 12 reps or 8 to 10 reps, this may equate to a 5 or 10% increase in dumbbell weight to the exercise.

A small increase in weight added may actually decrease the specified amount of reps allocated. This is when you gain a good understanding of your true training repetition range adapted into a strength cycle. Hence, when 12 repetitions of one exercise become easy for the 2-3 sets completed, a 5% increase maybe added at your next training session. This 5% increase may result in a smaller amount of repetitions being performed in the final set, but that's okay because this is when the body really starts to work. The idea is to stay with this weight until this too becomes easy, then increase the weight again in small increments. These ongoing changes never allow the body to adapt and changes in body shape and muscle tone will occur.

A basic beginner's routine consists of 1 to 3 sets for each major muscle group, with 10 to 15 reps performed per set. Between sets you rest for approximately 60-90 seconds, until you feel ready to tackle the exercise again. You'll require longer rests of 180 seconds or more between sets of more complex or higher intensity power exercises in the future. The rest period is also a great time to stretch or complete less strenuous exercises such as training the abdominal region to help maximize training time and drink some water to replenish the body.

Another rule of thumb in terms of rest relates to the amount of time before training the same muscle group again. It is recommended that once reps of less than 8-10 are being used at least 48-72 hours of rest time is required before training the same muscle groups again. Various research suggests that training programs should limit periods of complete inactivity to no more than two to three weeks. Prolonged periods of inactivity should be avoided and the training program should incorporate some form of body maintenance training where a prolonged break is desired.

Training Progression

Prior to starting any exercise in your program, always perform a very light warm-up set of the exercise to prepare you physically and mentally. Beginners should use slow, controlled movements with a continuous flow when starting out until all reps are completed. This keeps the muscle under tension for the whole set and is where real strength gains occur. Over many months of training, the speed and power of the movement will increase due to the amount of weight being lifted. As a result, the neuromuscular function will also improve resulting in better muscle coordination and an increase in one's metabolic rate that leans up muscle tissue and burns fat more effectively.

When you are first starting out and figuring out what size dumbbell weights are good for you, you'll have to go through some trial and error to find the correct weight. The 10 to 15 repetition range is based on the principle that beginners should use slightly lower weight for the first month, in order to allow their connective tissue, muscles and nervous system time to adapt to the loading and learn each exercise with good form.

Body Coach® Strength Training System

To assist in the development of strength training, for those who are looking for a simple training model to follow I have developed the Body Coach® Strength Training System for the Upper and Lower Body Regions. The concept behind this system relates to having a program that targets all major muscle groups of the body yet allows you to pick and choose the exercises to perform from a selection supplied, or more if necessary. This provides you with plenty of variety as well as options when going to the gym or training at home. Additional dumbbell exercises may be included.

Body Coach® Strength Training System Guidelines:

- Choose 2 exercises from each muscle group in upper body, or only 1 exercise in various lower body exercises. For example, choose two chest exercises from the list, such as:

  - CHEST: 1. Dumbbell Bench Press; 2: Flat Bench Flyes
- Perform 4 sets of 10-12 reps (12, 12, 10, 10) with 60 seconds rest between sets
- 4-week training cycle: 3 days per week (i.e. Mon, Wed, Fri)

	Training Day 1	Training Day 2	Training Day 3
Week 1	Upper Body	Lower Body	Upper Body
Week 2	Lower Body	Upper Body	Lower Body
Week 3	Upper Body	Lower Body	Upper Body
Week 4	Lower Body	Upper Body	Lower Body

- 4-week training cycle: 2 days a week: Day 1: Upper Body; Day 2: Lower Body
- The 12-week – 4 week Strength Training cycles include:

  Week 1 – 4:   4 sets of 12, 12 , 10, 10 repetitions

  Week 5 – 8:   4 sets of 10, 10, 8, 8 repetitions

  Week 9 – 12:   4 sets of 8, 8 , 6, 6 repetitions

As you progress through each cycle, a decrease in repetitions generally means an increase in weight. For instance, the weight you can lift for eight repetitions should be considerably heavier than what you can lift for ten.

Body Coach® Upper Body Strength Training System

	Exercise List	Reps			Sets	Rest
		W1-4	W5-8	W9-12		
Chest	1. Flat Bench Fly	12	10	8	4	60-90
	2. Incline Bench Fly	12	10	8		sec
	3. Fitness Ball Flyes	10	8	6		
	4. Flat Bench Press	10	8	6		
	5. Decline Bench Press					
	6. Incline Bench Press					
Back	1. Double Arm Row	12	10	8	4	60-90
	2. Bent Over Flyes	12	10	8		sec
	3. High Bench Rows	10	8	6		
	4. Single Arm Row	10	8	6		
	5. Pullovers					
	6. Upright Rows – Close Grip					
Shoulders	1. Reverse Fly	12	10	8	4	60-90
	2. Front Raise – Both Arms	12	10	8		sec
	3. Front Raise – Alternate Arms	10	8	6		
	4. Seated Shoulder Press	10	8	6		
	5. Seated Arnold Press					
	6. Lateral Raise					
Biceps	1. Open Curl	12	10	8	4	60-90
	2. Rotation Curl	12	10	8		sec
	3. Alternate Arm Curl	10	8	6		
	4. Hammer Curls	10	8	6		
	5. Seated Curls					
	6. Concentration Curls					
Triceps	1. Two-hand Bent Over Kickback	12	10	8	4	60-90
	2. Flat Bench Extensions	12	10	8		sec
	3. Flat Bench Single Arm Extension	10	8	6		
	4. Incline Extensions	10	8	6		
	5. Incline Single Arm Extension					
	6. Standing Single Dumbbell					

Note:
- Choose 2 exercises for each muscle group.
- For variation, add additional exercises for each muscle group, if necessary.
- Weeks 1 – 4 apply a 3:1:2 lifting tempo; rest for 60 seconds between sets.
- Weeks 5 – 8 apply a 2:1:1 lifting tempo; resting for up 90 seconds between sets.
- Weeks 9 – 12 apply 2:0:1 resting for up 90 seconds between sets.

Body Coach® Lower Body Strength Training System

	Exercise List		Reps			Sets	Rest
	Choose 2 Exercises	W1-4	W5-8	W9-12			
Thigh/Butt	1. Squat	12	10	8		4	60-90
	2. Sumo Squat	12	10	8			sec
	3. Overhead Squat	10	8	6			
	4. Fitness Ball Squat	10	8	6			
	5. Stationary Lunge						
	6. Alternate Leg Lunge						
Hamstrings	Choose 1 Exercise						
	1. Straight-Leg Deadlift	12	10	8		4	60-90
	2. Single-Leg Deadlift	12	10	8			sec
	3. Good Morning	10	8	6			
	4. Step Ups	10	8	6			
	5. Single-Leg Drives						
Calves	Choose 1 Exercise						
	1. Seated Calf Raise	12	10	8		4	60-90
	2. Standing Calf Raise	12	10	8			sec
	3. Fitness Ball Wall Calf Raises	10	8	6			
	4. Balance Calf-Raise	10	8	6			

Core & Abs

10 Minute Workout:
1. Body Dish
2. Toe Touch
3. Abdominal Crunch Series
4. Fitness Ball Crunch Series
5. Collins-Lateral Fly™
6. Lateral Side Raises

Note: The core abdominal region plays a key role in posture and muscular synergy between the upper and lower body. As a result, spend 10 minutes performing exercises to strengthen this region using:
(a) Time on task (i.e. 30 seconds); or
(b) Repetition Ratio - 3:1:1

Note:
- Choose 2 exercises for each muscle group.
- For variation, add additional exercises for each muscle group, if necessary.
- Weeks 1 – 4 apply a 3:1:2 lifting tempo; rest for 60 seconds between sets.
- Weeks 5 – 8 apply a 2:1:1 lifting tempo; resting for up 90 seconds between sets.
- Weeks 9 – 12 apply 2:0:1 resting for up 90 seconds between sets.

20-Week Strength Training Cycle

The following 20-week strength training cycle is progressive in nature and is aimed and taking you through a journey – developing general strength before building muscle and then maximizing strength gains and transferring this into power. This 20-week cycle will help shape the way you train in the future by getting to know how your body and mind work together and respond to the training stimulus at hand. This is because this program provides you with a benchmark training framework for you to follow.

As you will discover through regular participation, this training cycle can be modified and adapted to suit your specific training needs – as the ultimate combination of reps, sets, tempo and exercises for each individual will vary as well as the force being generated through the mass being lifted and acceleration of each lift itself. Each stage of the 20-week program needs to be completed in the specified order to get the maximum benefit. So I implore you to go into this 20-week training cycle with a positive mind-set towards practical learning from which you can adapt any future training and modifications using a similar 'framework' to suit your specific needs.

Training Overview

The program is based on two programs (A & B) for each training phase which are alternated each time you train. The number of times you perform these will depend upon your training schedule and availability each week. As a result, I have provided 2, 3 and 4 day training models.

Each program is set out with the respective weeks at the top of the program. For example; if you can only train 2 days a week then this may entail Monday and Thursdays; 3 days a week – Monday, Wednesday and Friday; or 4 days a week – Monday, Tuesday, Thursday, Friday or similar. The training cycle requires you to complete all the specified sets of one exercise before moving onto the next exercise as this will help you achieve the goals of the program.

To achieve the most from your training, it is recommended that on your last set of any given exercise, you lift the heaviest weight possible for that number of repetitions. If you can complete all the repetitions specified in your last set, then you may need to increase the weights by 2.5 to 5%. As you progress through each cycle, a decrease in repetitions generally means an increase in weight. For instance, the weight you can lift for eight repetitions should be considerably heavier than what you can lift for ten. On some occasions though, the weight may be similar depending on the lifting tempo or the speed at which you perform the various phases of an exercise, so adapt accordingly. Here's one example of this using a dumbbell bench press exercise when changing stages:

Stage: Hypertrophy
Exercise: Dumbbell Bench Press
Lifting Tempo: 3:1:3 – lower the dumbbells over a count of three seconds, pause for one second and then lift the weight up again over three seconds.
Stage: Strength
Exercise: Dumbbell Bench Press
Lifting Tempo: 2:1:1 – lower the dumbbells over a count of two seconds, pause for one second and then explode the weight up as fast as possible.

The time you take between sets is dependent on the program you are undertaking. Throughout each stage the following rest between sets is recommended.

- General Preparation: 60-90 seconds
- Hypertrophy: 90 seconds
- Max. Strength and Power: More than 180 seconds (3 minutes+)

Training Tables

2 Training Sessions per Week

Week	1		2		3		4	
Session	1	2	1	2	1	2	1	2
Program	A	B	A	B	A	B	A	B

3 Training Sessions per Week

Week	1			2			3			4		
Session	1	2	3	1	2	3	1	2	3	1	2	3
Program	A	B	A	B	A	B	A	B	A	B	A	B

4 Training Sessions per Week

Week	1				2				3				4			
Session	1	2	3	4	1	2	3	4	1	2	3	4	1	2	3	4
Program	A	B	A	B	A	B	A	B	A	B	A	B	A	B	A	B

Training Program

Refer to training tables for application to 2, 3 or 4 sessions a week in the following stages in terms of performing Programs A or B

Stage 1 (weeks 1–4): General Preparation

Program A	Program B	Sets x Reps	Tempo	Rest (secs)
Squat	Bench Press	3 x 15	2:1:2	60-90
High Bench Rows	Incline Bench Press	3 x 15	2:1:2	60-90
Sumo Deadlift	Single Arm Rows	3 x 15	2:1:2	60-90
Reverse Fly	Seated Shoulder Press	3 x 15	2:1:2	60-90
Stationary Lunge	Upright Rows	3 x 15	2:1:2	60-90
Open Curl	Lateral Raises	3 x 15	2:1:2	60-90
Toe Touch	Incline Extensions	3 x 15	2:1:2	60-90

Stage 2 (weeks 5–8): Hypertrophy

Program A	Program B	Sets x Reps	Tempo	Rest (secs)
Dead Lifts	Incline Bench Press	3 x 12	3:1:3	90
Front Squats	Dumbbell Chest Flyes	3 x 12	3:1:3	90
Stationary Lunges	Seated Shoulder Press	3 x 12	3:1:3	90
Pullovers	Lateral Raises	3 x 12	3:1:3	90
Double Arm Row	Incline Extension	3 x 12	3:1:3	90
Rotation Curl	Close Grip Push-ups	3 x 12	3:1:3	90
Alternate Arm Curl	Back Raises	3 x 12	3:1:3	90

Stage 3 (weeks 9–12): Strength

Program A	Program B	Sets x Reps	Tempo	Rest (secs)
Single Leg Deadlifts	Bench Press	4 x 10	2:1:2	90-120
Front Squats	Incline Bench Press	4 x 10	2:1:2	90-120
Single Leg Squat	Seated Shoulder Press	4 x 10	2:1:2	90-120
High Bench Rows	Lateral Raises	4 x 10	2:1:2	90-120
Single Arm Row	Upright Row	4 x 10	2:1:2	90-120
Hammer Curls	Standing Two Arm Ext.	4 x 10	2:1:2	90-120

Stage 4 (weeks 13–16): Strength Conversion

Program A	Program B	Sets x Reps	Tempo	Rest (secs)
High Pulls	Split Jerk	4 x 6	Explosive	180+
Push Press	Bench Press	4 x 6	2:1:1	180+
Bent Over Rows	Incline Flyes	4 x 6	2:1:1	180+
Step-Ups	2+1 Military Press	4 x 6	2:1:1	180+
Squats	Lateral Raises	4 x 6	2:1:1	180+
Single Arm Rows	Lying Triceps Extension	4 x 6	2:1:1	180+

Stage 5 (weeks 17–20): Power Conversion

Program A	Program B	Sets x Reps	Tempo	Rest (secs)
High Pulls	Power Cleans	4 x 3	Explosive	180+
Push Press	Snatch	4 x 3	Explosive	180+
Deadlift	Squat	4 x 3	2:1:1	180+
High Bench Pulls	Bench Press	4 x 3	2:1:1	180+

Note: Abdominal exercises are performed in addition to this training program.

Dynamic Dumbbell Training Overview

Ultimately, there are multiple training cycles and strength and power training methods that can be applied. My goal as a coach has been to provide you with a practical strength foundation to build upon in the future. Athletes and gym enthusiasts who participate in this program will gain both the theoretical and practical knowledge and understanding for optimal strength and power gains, allowing them to adapt this to best suit their training needs. Think of it like learning how to drive with the assistance of a driving instructor. The more you practice, improve and learn along the way, the more aware and better you'll become. Once you gain that valuable experience and start to improve your technique and spatial awareness, with confidence, you'll improve in all areas of your training. In transferring this vision to Dynamic Dumbbell Training you will have gained the vital practical experience to adapt a specific training plan to suit you in the future.

My personal goal was helping you reach this point. I have enjoyed working with you and wish you all the best with your future training.
Paul Collins
The Body Coach®
Australia's Personal Trainer™
www.thebodycoach.com

Dynamic Dumbbell Training Exercise Index

Body Coach® Education, Training & Products

Join The Body Coach® Paul Collins, international author and Strength and Conditioning Coach and his team of experts in the Fastfeet® Speed for Sport Training clinics, workshops, camps, seminars and coaching for all sports.

Paul Presenting at International Fitness conference, Sydney, Australia

Paul Collins and Ron Palmer Presenting Speed for Sport Coaching Seminar

For more details and products visit the following websites:
www.thebodycoach.com
www.bodycoach.com.au
www.fastfeet.com.au